THE
STORY OF
MY
LIFE

As Told
By
Jesus Christ

THE
STORY OF
MY
LIFE

As Told
By
Jesus Christ

The Story of My Life as Told by Jesus Christ

Copyright
MCMXCIX
Published by
SEEDSOWERS
Publishing House

Published by
SEEDSOWERS
Christian Books Publishing House
PO Box 3317
Jacksonville, FL 32206
(800) 228-2665
www.SeedSowers.com

Library of Congress Cataloging-In-Publication Data
ISBN 0-940232-71-5
1. Religious
2. Non-fiction

Zechariah (9)(17)
Herod (9)-21-27
Elizabeth (9)(13)(17)
Aaron (9)
John (9)(17)
Elijah (9)
Gabiel (9)(13)
Mary (13)-21-22-27
Joseph (13)-21-22-27
Jesus (13)-22-27
David (13)-21
Israel (14)
Abraham (14)
Augustus (21)
Quirinius (21)
Simeon (22)
Anna (22)
Shepherds
Wise men 27
Archelaus 28
(Herod's son)

*Here begins the Good News about
Jesus the Messiah,
the Son of God . . .*

Mk. 1:1

PROLOGUE

PROLOGUE

In the beginning I, the Word, already existed. I was with God, and I was God.

I was in the beginning with God. I created everything there is. Nothing exists that I didn't make. Life itself was in me, and my life gives light to everyone. My light shines through the darkness, and the darkness can never extinguish it.

Although the world was made through me, the world did not recognize me when I came. Even in my own land and among my own people, I was not accepted. But to all who believed me and accepted me, I gave the right to become children of God. They are reborn! This is not a physical birth resulting from human passion or plan—this rebirth comes from God. So I became human and lived here on the earth among you. I am full of unfailing love and faithfulness. And you have seen my glory, the glory of the only Son of the Father.

Jo. 1:1-5, 10-14

3

PART I

MY EARLY YEARS
ON
EARTH

THE
BIRTH OF
MY COUSIN JOHN
FORETOLD
6 BC

The Birth of John the Baptist Foretold

6 BC   The Temple in Jerusalem

It all begins with a Jewish priest, Zechariah, who lived when Herod was king of Judea.

Zechariah was a member of the priestly order of Abijah. His wife, Elizabeth, was also from the priestly line of Aaron. Zechariah and Elizabeth were righteous in God's eyes, careful to obey all of the Lord's commandments and regulations.

They had no children because Elizabeth was barren, and now they were both very old.

One day Zechariah was serving God in the Temple, for his order was on duty that week. As was the custom of the priests, he was chosen by lot to enter the sanctuary and burn incense in the Lord's presence. While the incense was being burned, a great crowd stood outside, praying.

Zechariah was in the sanctuary when an angel of the Lord appeared, standing to the right of the incense altar. Zechariah was overwhelmed with fear.

But the angel said, "Don't be afraid, Zechariah! God has heard your prayer, and your wife, Elizabeth, will bear you a son! And you are to name him John. You will have great joy and gladness, and many will rejoice with you at his birth, for he will be great in the eyes of the Lord. He must never touch wine or hard liquor, and he will be filled with the Holy Spirit, even before his birth. And he will persuade many Israelites to turn to the Lord their God. He will be a man with the spirit and power of Elijah, the prophet of old. He will precede the coming of the Lord, preparing the people for his arrival. He will turn the hearts of the fathers to their children, and he will change disobedient minds to accept godly wisdom."

Zechariah said to the angel, "How can I know this will happen? I'm an old man now, and my wife is also well along in years."

Then the angel said, "I am Gabriel! I stand in the very presence of God. It was he who sent me to bring you this good news! And now, since you didn't believe what I said, you won't be able to speak until the child is born. For my words will certainly come true at the proper time."

Meanwhile, the people were waiting for Zechariah to come out, wondering why he was taking so long. When he finally did come out, he couldn't speak to them. Then they realized from his gestures that he must have seen a vision in the Temple sanctuary.

He stayed at the Temple until his term of service was over, and then he returned home. Soon afterward his wife, Elizabeth, became

9

pregnant and went into seclusion for five months. "How kind the Lord is!" she exclaimed. "He has taken away my disgrace of having no children!"

Lu. 1:5-25

MY
BIRTH
FORETOLD

5 BC

My Mother Encounters an Angel

In the sixth month of Elizabeth's pregnancy, God sent the angel Gabriel to Nazareth, a village in Galilee, to a virgin named Mary. She was engaged to be married to a man named Joseph, a descendant of King David.

Gabriel appeared to her and said, "Greetings, favored woman! The Lord is with you!"

Confused and disturbed, Mary tried to think what the angel could mean. "Don't be frightened, Mary," the angel told her, "for God has decided to bless you! You will become pregnant and have a son, and you are to name him Jesus. He will be very great and will be called the Son of the Most High. And the Lord God will give him the throne of his ancestor David. And he will reign over Israel forever; his Kingdom will never end!"

Mary asked the angel, "But how can I have a baby? I am a virgin." The angel replied, "The Holy Spirit will come upon you, and the power of the Most High will overshadow you. So the baby born to you will be holy, and he will be called the Son of God. What's more, your relative Elizabeth has become pregnant in her old age! People used to say she was barren, but she is already in her sixth month. For nothing is impossible with God."

Mary responded, "I am the Lord's servant, and I am willing to accept whatever he wants. May everything you have said come true." And then the angel left.

My mother, Mary, was engaged to be married to Joseph. But while she was still a virgin, she became pregnant by the Holy Spirit. Joseph, her fiancé, being a just man, decided to break the engagement quietly, so as not to disgrace her publicly.

As Joseph considered this, he fell asleep, and the angel of the Lord appeared to him in a dream. "Joseph, son of David," the angel said, "do not be afraid to go ahead with your marriage to Mary. For the child within her has been conceived by the Holy Spirit. And she will have a son, and you are to name him Jesus, for he will save his people from their sins."

All of this happened to fulfill the Lord's message through his prophet:

> *Look! The virgin will conceive a child! She will give birth to a son, and he will be called Emmanuel (meaning, God is with us).*

Isa. 7:14, 8:8, 10

13

When Joseph woke up, he did what the angel of the Lord commanded. He brought Mary home to be his wife, but she remained a virgin until I was born. And Joseph named me Jesus.

Mt. 1:18b-25; Lu. 1:26-38

My Mother's Visit to Elizabeth

The hill country of Judea

A few days later Mary hurried to the hill country of Judea, to the town where Zechariah lived.

She entered the house and greeted Elizabeth. At the sound of Mary's greeting, Elizabeth's child leaped within her, and Elizabeth was filled with the Holy Spirit.

Elizabeth gave a glad cry and exclaimed to Mary,

You are blessed by God above all other women, and your child is blessed. What an honor this is, that the mother of my Lord should visit me! When you came in and greeted me, my baby jumped for joy the instant I heard your voice! You are blessed, because you believed that the Lord would do what he said.

My mother responded,

Oh, how I praise the Lord. How I rejoice in God my Savior! For he took notice of this lowly servant girl, and now generation after generation will call me blessed. For he, the Mighty One, is holy, and he has done great things for me. His mercy goes on from generation to generation, to all who fear him. His mighty arm does tremendous things! How he scatters the proud and haughty ones! He has taken princes from their thrones and exalted the lowly. He has satisfied the hungry with good things and sent the rich away with empty hands. And how he has helped his servant Israel! He has not forgotten his promise to be merciful. For he promised our ancestors—Abraham and his children—to be merciful to them forever.

Mary stayed with Elizabeth about three months and then went back to her own home.

Lu. 1:39-56

14

THE
BIRTH OF
MY COUSIN
JOHN

5 BC

John's Birth

Now it was time for Elizabeth's baby to be born, and it was a boy. The word spread quickly to her neighbors and relatives that the Lord had been very kind to her, and everyone rejoiced with her. When the baby was eight days old, all the relatives and friends came for the circumcision ceremony. They wanted to name him Zechariah, after his father.

But Elizabeth said, "No! His name is John!"

"What?" they exclaimed. "There is no one in all your family by that name."

So they asked the baby's father, communicating to him by making gestures. Zechariah motioned for a writing tablet, and to everyone's surprise he wrote, "His name is John!" Instantly Zechariah could speak again, and he began praising God.

Wonder fell upon the whole neighborhood, and the news of what had happened spread throughout the Judean hills. Everyone who heard about it reflected on these events and asked, "I wonder what this child will turn out to be? For the hand of the Lord is surely upon him in a special way."

Then his father, Zechariah, was filled with the Holy Spirit and gave this prophecy:

Praise the Lord, the God of Israel, because he has visited his people and redeemed them. He has sent us a mighty Savior from the royal line of his servant David, just as he promised through his holy prophets long ago. Now we will be saved from our enemies and from all who hate us. He has been merciful to our ancestors by remembering his sacred covenant with them, the covenant he gave to our ancestor Abraham. We have been rescued from our enemies, so we can serve God without fear, in holiness and righteousness forever. And you, my little son, will be called the prophet of the Most High, because you will prepare the way for the Lord. You will tell his people how to find salvation through forgiveness of their sins. Because of God's tender mercy, the light from heaven is about to break upon us, to give light to those who sit in darkness and in the shadow of death, and to guide us to the path of peace.

John grew up and became strong in spirit. Then he lived in the wilderness until he began his public ministry to Israel.

God sent John to tell everyone about the light so that everyone might believe because of John's testimony. John himself was not the light; he was only a witness to the light. The one who is the true light, who gives light to everyone, was going to come into the world.

Lu. 1:57-80; Jo. 1:6-9

MY
BIRTH
4BC

The City of David, My Birth Place

4 BC   Bethlehem, in a manger

Now, this is how Jesus, the Messiah, was born . . .

I was born in the town of Bethlehem in Judea, during the reign of King Herod. At that time the Roman emperor, Augustus, decreed that a census should be taken throughout the Roman Empire. (This was the first census taken when Quirinius was governor of Syria.) All returned to their own towns to register for this census. And because Joseph was a descendant of King David, he had to go to Bethlehem in Judea, David's ancient home. He traveled there from the village of Nazareth in Galilee. He took with him my mother (his fiancée) who was obviously pregnant by this time.

And while they were there, the time came for me to be born. Mary gave birth to me, her first child, a son. She wrapped me snugly in strips of cloth and laid me in a manger, because there was no room for us in the village inn.

That night some shepherds were in the fields outside the village, guarding their flocks of sheep. Suddenly, an angel of the Lord appeared among them, and the radiance of the Lord's glory surrounded them. They were terribly frightened, but the angel reassured them. "Don't be afraid!" he said. "I bring you good news of great joy for everyone! The Savior—yes, the Messiah, the Lord— has been born tonight in Bethlehem, the city of David! And this is how you will recognize him: You will find a baby lying in a manger, wrapped snugly in strips of cloth!"

Suddenly, the angel was joined by a vast host of others—the armies of heaven—praising God:

> *Glory to God in the highest heavens, and*
> *peace on earth to all whom God favors.*

When the angels had returned to heaven, the shepherds said to each other, "Come on, let's go to Bethlehem! Let's see this wonderful thing that has happened, which the Lord has told us about."

They ran to the village and found Mary and Joseph. And there I was, lying in the manger. Then the shepherds told everyone what had happened and what the angel had said to them about me. All who heard the shepherds' story were astonished, but Mary quietly treasured these things in her heart and thought about them often.

The shepherds went back to their fields and flocks, glorifying and praising God for what the angels had told them, and because they had seen me, just as the angel had said.

Eight days later, when I was circumcised, I was named Jesus, the name given to me by the angel even before I was conceived.

Mt. 1:18a, 2:1a; Lu. 2:1-21

Simeon and Anna Were Waiting for Me

Jerusalem, at the Temple

Then it was time for the purification offering, as required by the law of Moses after the birth of a child; so my parents took me to Jerusalem to present me to the Lord. The law of the Lord says,

> *If a woman's first child is a boy, he must be dedicated to the Lord.*

Exodus 13:2

So they offered a sacrifice according to what was required in the law of the Lord—

> *either a pair of turtle doves or two young pigeons.*

Lev. 12:8

Now there was a man named Simeon who lived in Jerusalem. He was a righteous man and very devout. He was filled with the Holy Spirit, and he eagerly expected the Messiah to come and rescue Israel. The Holy Spirit had revealed to him that he would not die until he had seen the Lord's Messiah. That day the Spirit led him to the Temple. So when Mary and Joseph came to present me to the Lord as the law required, Simeon was there.

He took me in his arms and praised God, saying,

> Lord, now I can die in peace! As you promised me, I have seen the Savior you have given to all people. He is a light to reveal God to the nations, and he is the glory of your people Israel!

Joseph and my mother were amazed at what was being said about me.

Then Simeon blessed them, and he said to my mother,

> This child will be rejected by many in Israel, and it will be their undoing. But he will be the greatest joy to many others. Thus, the deepest thoughts of many hearts will be revealed. And a sword will pierce your very soul.

Anna, a prophet, was also there in the Temple. She was the daughter of Phanuel, of the tribe of Asher, and was very old. She was a widow, for her husband had died when they had been married only seven years. She was now eighty-four years old. She never left the Temple but stayed there day and night, worshiping God with fasting and prayer. She came along just as Simeon was talking with my mother and Joseph, and she began praising God. She talked about me to everyone who had been waiting for the promised King to come and deliver Jerusalem.

Lu. 2:22-38

A
VISIT FROM MEN
OF THE EAST
3 BC

Men from Babylon Traveled a Long Way to Worship Me

3 BC   Jerusalem and Nazareth

My parents fulfilled all the requirements of the law of the Lord and returned home to Nazareth in Galilee.

About that time some wise men from eastern lands arrived in Jerusalem, asking, "Where is the newborn king of the Jews? We have seen his star as it arose, and we have come to worship him."

Herod was deeply disturbed by their question, as was all of Jerusalem. He called a meeting of the leading priests and teachers of religious law. "Where did the prophets say the Messiah would be born?" he asked them. "In Bethlehem," they said, "for this is what the prophet wrote:

> *O Bethlehem of Judah, you are not just a lowly village in Judah, for a ruler will come from you who will be the shepherd for my people Israel.*
>
> Mic. 5:2; 2 Sam. 5:2

Then Herod sent a private message to the wise men, asking them to come see him. At this meeting he learned the exact time when they first saw the star. Then he told them, "Go to Bethlehem and search carefully for the child. And when you find him, come back and tell me so that I can go and worship him, too!"

After this interview the wise men went their way. Once again the star appeared to them, guiding them to Bethlehem. It went ahead of them and stopped over the place where I was. When they saw the star, they were filled with joy! They entered the house where my mother, Mary, and I were, and they fell down before me and worshiped me. Then they opened their treasure chests and gave me gifts of gold, frankincense, and myrrh. But when it was time to leave, they went home another way, because God had warned them in a dream not to return to Herod.

Mt. 2:1b-12; Lu. 2:39

My Escape into Egypt

After the wise men were gone, an angel of the Lord appeared to Joseph in a dream. "Get up and flee to Egypt with the child and his mother," the angel said. "Stay there until I tell you to return, because Herod is going to try to kill the child." That night Joseph left for Egypt with me and Mary, my mother, and we stayed there until

Herod's death. This fulfilled what the Lord had spoken through the prophet:

I called my Son out of Egypt.

Hos. 11:1

Herod was furious when he learned that the wise men had outwitted him. He sent soldiers to kill all the boys in and around Bethlehem who were two years old and under, because the wise men had told him the star first appeared to them about two years earlier. Herod's brutal action fulfilled the prophecy of Jeremiah:

A cry of anguish is heard in Ramah—weeping and mourning unrestrained. Rachel weeps for her children, refusing to be comforted, for they are dead.

Jer. 31:15

When Herod died, an angel of the Lord appeared in a dream to Joseph in Egypt and told him, "Get up and take the child and his mother back to the land of Israel, because those who were trying to kill the child are dead."

So Joseph returned immediately to Israel with my mother and me. But when he learned that the new ruler was Herod's son Archelaus, he was afraid. Then, in another dream, he was warned to go to Galilee. So we went and lived in a town called Nazareth. This fulfilled what was spoken by the prophets concerning the Messiah: "He will be called a Nazarene."

There I grew up healthy and strong. I was filled with wisdom beyond my years, and God placed his special favor upon me.

Mt. 2:13-23; Lu. 2:40

AN
INCIDENT
IN MY
CHILDHOOD

AD 8

I Reasoned with Religious Teachers

Spring, AD 8   Jerusalem, at the Temple

Every year my parents went to Jerusalem for the Passover festival. When I was twelve years old, we attended the festival as usual.

After the celebration was over, they started home to Nazareth, but I stayed behind in Jerusalem. My parents didn't miss me at first, because they assumed I was with friends among the other travelers. But when I didn't show up that evening, they started to look for me among our relatives and friends. When they couldn't find me, they went back to Jerusalem to search for me there.

Three days later they finally discovered me. I was in the Temple, sitting among the religious teachers, discussing deep questions with them. And all who heard me were amazed at my understanding and my answers. My parents didn't know what to think. "Son!" my mother said to me. "Why have you done this to us? Your father and I have been frantic, searching for you everywhere."

"But why did you need to search?" I asked. "You should have known that I would be in my Father's house." But they didn't understand what I meant. *TEMPLE*.

Then I returned to Nazareth with them and was obedient to them; and my mother stored all these things in her heart. So I grew both in height and in wisdom, and I was loved by God and by all who knew me.

Lu. 2:41-52

STORED
TREASURED
KEPT
PONDER

MY
GENEALOGY

Joseph's Ancestry

This is a record of the ancestors of
Jesus the Messiah,
a descendant of King David
and of Abraham:

Abraham was the father of Isaac.

Isaac was the father of Jacob.

Jacob was the father of Judah and his brothers.

Judah was the father of Perez and Zerah (their mother was Tamar).

Perez was the father of Hezron.

Hezron was the father of Ram.

Ram was the father of Amminadab.

Amminadab was the father of Nahshon.

Nahshon was the father of Salmon.

Salmon was the father of Boaz (his mother was Rahab).

Boaz was the father of Obed (his mother was Ruth).

Obed was the father of Jesse.

Jesse was the father of David.

David was the father of Solomon (his mother was Bathsheba, the widow of Uriah).

Solomon was the father of Rehoboam.

Rehoboam was the father of Abijah.

Abijah was the father of Asaph.

Asaph was the father of Jehoshaphat.

Jehoshaphat was the father of Jehoram.

Jehoram was the father of Uzziah.

Uzziah was the father of Jotham.

Jotham was the father of Ahaz.

Ahaz was the father of Hezekiah.

Hezekiah was the father of Manasseh.

Manasseh was the father of Amos.

Amos was the father of Josiah.

Josiah was the father of Jehoiachin and his brothers (born at the time of the exile of Babylon).

After the Babylonian exile:

Jehoiachin was the father of Shealtiel.

Shealtiel was the father of Zerubbabel.

Zerubbabel was the father of Abiud.

Abiud was the father of Eliakim.

Eliakim was the father of Azor.

Azor was the father of Zadok.

Zadok was the father of Akim.

Akim was the father of Eliud.

Eliud was the father of Eleazar.
Eleazar was the father of Matthan.
Matthan was the father of Jacob.
Jacob was the father of Joseph, the husband of Mary.
Mary was the mother of Jesus.
I am Jesus, who is called the Messiah.

All those listed above include fourteen generations from Abraham to King David, and fourteen from David's time to the Babylonian exile, and fourteen from the Babylonian exile to the Messiah.

Mt. 1:1-17

My Mother's Ancestry

I was known as the son of Joseph.
Joseph was the son of Heli.
Heli was the son of Matthat.
Matthat was the son of Levi.
Levi was the son of Melki.
Melki was the son of Jannai.
Jannai was the son of Joseph.
Joseph was the son of Mattathias.
Mattathias was the son of Amos.
Amos was the son of Nahum.
Nahum was the son of Esli.
Esli was the son of Naggai.
Naggai was the son of Maath.
Maath was the son of Mattathias.
Mattathias was the son of Semein.
Semein was the son of Josech.
Josech was the son of Joda.
Joda was the son of Joanan.
Joanan was the son of Rhesa.
Rhesa was the son of Zerubbabel.
Zerubbabel was the son of Shealtiel.
Shealtiel was the son of Neri.
Neri was the son of Melki.
Melki was the son of Addi.
Addi was the son of Cosam.
Cosam was the son of Elmadam.
Elamadam was the son of Er.
Er was the son of Joshua.
Joshua was the son of Eliezer.

Eliezer was the son of Jorim.
Jorim was the son of Matthat.
Matthat was the son of Levi.
Levi was the son of Simeon.
Simeon was the son of Judah.
Judah was the son of Joseph.
Joseph was the son of Jonam.
Jonam was the son of Eleakim.
Eliakim was the son of Melea.
Melea was the son of Menna.
Menna was the son of Mattatha.
Mattatha was the son of Nathan.
Nathan was the son of David.
David was the son of Jesse.
Jesse was the son of Obed.
Obed was the son of Boaz.
Boaz was the son of Salmon.
Salmon was the son of Nahshon.
Nahshon was the son of Amminadab.
Amminadab was the son of Admin.
Admin was the son of Arni.
Arni was the son of Hezron.
Hezron was the son of Perez.
Perez was the son of Judah.
Judah was the son of Jacob.
Jacob was the son of Isaac.
Isaac was the son of Abraham.
Abraham was the son of Terah.
Terah was the son of Nahor.
Nahor was the son of Serug.
Serug was the son of Reu.
Reu was the son of Peleg.
Peleg was the son of Eber.
Eber was the son of Shelah.
Shelah was the son of Cainan.
Cainan was the son of Arphaxad.
Arphaxad was the son of Shem.
Shem was the son of Noah.
Noah was the son of Lamech.
Lamech was the son of Methuselah.
Methuselah was the son of Enoch.
Enoch was the son of Jared.
Jared was the son of Mahalalel.

Mahalalel was the son of Kenan.
Kenan was the son of Enosh.
Enosh was the son of Seth.
Seth was the son of Adam.
Adam was the son of God.

Lu. 3:23b-38

*Nehemiah written
last book written*

400 yrs ... before Jesus

THE
BEGINNING OF
MY COUSIN JOHN'S
MINISTRY
AD 26

John's Ministry in the Wilderness

It was now the fifteenth year of the reign of Tiberius, the Roman emperor.

Pilate was governor over Judea; Herod Antipas was ruler over Galilee; his brother Philip was ruler over Iturea and Traconitis; Lysanias was ruler over Abilene. Annas and Caiaphas were the high priests.

At that time a message from God came to John, son of Zechariah, who was living in the wilderness. John's clothes were woven from camel hair, and he wore a leather belt. His food was locusts and wild honey.

In those days John began preaching in the Judean wilderness. His message was, "Turn from your sins and turn to God, because the Kingdom of Heaven is near." *REPENT*

In the book of the prophet Isaiah, God said,

> *Look, I am sending my messenger before you, and he will prepare your way.*
>
> Mal. 3:1

This messenger was John the Baptist. He went from place to place on both sides of the Jordan River, preaching that people should be baptized to show that they had turned from their sins and turned to God to be forgiven. *REPENTED*

Isaiah had spoken of John when he said, *ACTS 19:3*

> *He is a voice shouting in the wilderness: "Prepare a pathway for the Lord's coming! Make straight a road for him! Fill in the valleys, and level the mountains and hills! Straighten the curves, and smooth out the rough places! And then all people will see the salvation sent from God."* *PAVE THE WAY*
>
> Isa. 40:3-5

People from Jerusalem and from every section of Judea and from all over the Jordan Valley traveled out to the wilderness to see and hear him preach. And when they confessed their sins, he baptized them in the Jordan River.

But when he saw many Pharisees and Sadducees coming to be baptized, he denounced them.

Here is a sample of John's preaching to the crowds that came for baptism: "You brood of snakes!" he exclaimed. "Who warned you to flee God's coming judgment? Prove by the way you live that you have really turned from your sins and turned to God. Don't just say, 'We're safe—we're descendants of Abraham.' That proves nothing. God can change these stones here into children of Abraham.

41

Even now the ax of God's judgment is poised, ready to sever your roots. Yes, every tree that does not produce good fruit will be chopped down and thrown into the fire."

The crowd asked, "What should we do?"

John replied, "If you have two coats, give one to the poor. If you have food, share it with those who are hungry."

Even corrupt tax collectors came to be baptized and asked, "Teacher, what should we do?"

"Show your honesty," he replied. "Make sure you collect no more taxes than the Roman government requires you to."

"What should we do?" asked some soldiers.

John replied, "Don't extort money, and don't accuse people of things you know they didn't do. And be content with your pay."

Everyone was expecting the Messiah to come soon, and they were eager to know whether John might be the Messiah. John answered their questions by saying, "I baptize with water those who turn from their sins and turn to God. But someone is coming soon who is far greater than I am—so much greater that I am not even worthy to be his slave. He will baptize you with the Holy Spirit and with fire.

"He is ready to separate the chaff from the grain with his winnowing fork. Then he will clean up the threshing area, storing the grain in his barn but burning the chaff with never-ending fire."

John used many such warnings as he announced the Good News to the people.

Mt. 3:1-12; Mk. 1:2-8; Lu. 3:1-18

Jesus was baptized

I
WAS BAPTIZED
BY JOHN
AD 26

My Baptism in the Jordan

Late AD 26   Jordan River

One day when the crowds were being baptized, I came from Nazareth in Galilee to the Jordan River to be baptized by John.

But John didn't want to baptize me. "I am the one who needs to be baptized by you," he said. "So why are you coming to me?"

But I said, "It must be done, because we must do everything that is right." So then John baptized me in the Jordan River.

After my baptism, as I came up out of the water praying, the heavens split open and I saw the Holy Spirit of God descending like a dove and settling on me.* And a voice from heaven said,

> *You are my beloved Son, and I am fully pleased with you.*

Then, full of the Holy Spirit, I left the Jordan River.

Mt. 3:13-17; Mk. 1:9-11; Lu. 3:21-22, 4:1a

I Was Tempted in the Wilderness

Judea

Immediately, the Holy Spirit compelled me to go out into the wilderness among the wild animals to be tempted by the devil for forty days and forty nights.

I ate nothing all that time and became very hungry. Then the devil came and said to me, "If you are the Son of God, change this stone into a loaf of bread." But I said to him, "No! The Scriptures say,

> *People need more than bread for their life; they must feed on every word of God.*

Deut. 8:3

Next the devil took me to the peak of a very high mountain and, in a moment of time, showed me the nations of the world and all their glory. The devil told me, "I will give you the glory of these kingdoms and authority over them—because they are mine to give to anyone I please. I will give it all to you if you will only bow down and worship me."

"Get out of here, Satan," I replied, "for the Scriptures say,

> *You must worship the Lord your God; serve only him.*

Deut. 6:13

45

Then the devil took me to Jerusalem, to the highest point of the Temple and said, "If you are the Son of God, jump off! For the Scriptures say,

> *He orders his angels to protect and guard you. And they will hold you with their hands to keep you from striking your foot on a stone.*

> Ps. 91:11-12

I responded, "The Scriptures also say,

> *Do not test the Lord your God.*

> Deut. 6:16

Then the devil left me until the next opportunity came.

When the devil had finished tempting me, angels came and cared for me.

> Mt. 4:1-11; Mk. 1:12-13; Lu. 4:1b-13

PART II

THE
FIRST YEAR
OF MY
MINISTRY

AD 27

My Cousin John's Testimony
Concerning Me

This was the testimony of John the Baptist when the Jewish leaders sent priests and Temple assistants from Jerusalem to ask John whether he claimed to be the Messiah. He flatly denied it. "I am not the Messiah," he said.

"Well then, who are you?" They asked. "Are you Elijah?"

"No," he replied.

"Are you a prophet?"

"No."

"Then who are you? Tell us, so we can give an answer to those who sent us. What do you have to say about yourself?"

John replied in the words of Isaiah:

> *I am a voice shouting in the wilderness, "Prepare a straight pathway for the Lord's coming!"*
>
> Isa. 40:3

Then those who were sent by the Pharisees asked him, "If you aren't the Messiah or Elijah or the Prophet, what right do you have to baptize?" John told them, "I baptize with water, but right here in the crowd is someone you do not know, who will soon begin his ministry. I am not even worthy to be his slave."

John pointed me out to the people. He shouted to the crowds, "This is the one I was talking about when I said, 'Someone is coming who is far greater than I am, for he existed long before I did.'"

This incident took place at Bethany, a village east of the Jordan River, where John was baptizing.

The next day John saw me coming toward him and said, "Look! There is the Lamb of God who takes away the sin of the world! He is the one I was talking about when I said, 'Soon a man is coming who is far greater than I am, for he existed long before I did.' I didn't know he was the one, but I have been baptizing with water in order to point him out to Israel."

Then John said, "I saw the Holy Spirit descending like a dove from heaven and resting upon him. I didn't know he was the one, but when God sent me to baptize with water, he told me, 'When you see the Holy Spirit descending and resting upon someone, he is the one you are looking for. He is the one who baptizes with the Holy Spirit.' I saw this happen to Jesus, so I testify that he is the Son of God."

Jo. 1:15, 19-34

49

My Earliest Followers

The following day, John was again standing with two of his disciples. As I walked by, John looked at me and then declared, "Look! There is the Lamb of God!" Then John's two disciples turned and followed me.

I looked around and saw them following. "What do you want?" I asked them.

They replied, "Rabbi" (which means Teacher), "where are you staying?"

"Come and see," I said.

It was about four o'clock in the afternoon when they went with me to the place, and we stayed there the rest of the day.

Andrew, Simon Peter's brother, was one of these men who had heard what John said and then followed me. The first thing Andrew did was to find his brother, Simon, and tell him, "We have found the Messiah" (which means the Christ).

Then Andrew brought Simon to meet me. Looking intently at Simon, I said, "You are Simon, the son of John—but you will be called Cephas" (which means Peter).

The next day I decided to go to Galilee.

I found Philip and said to him, "Come, be my disciple." Philip was from Bethsaida, Andrew and Peter's hometown.

Philip went off to look for Nathanael and told him, "We have found the very person Moses and the prophets wrote about! His name is Jesus, the son of Joseph from Nazareth."

"Nazareth!" exclaimed Nathanael, "Can anything good come from there?"

"Just come and see for yourself," Philip said.

As they approached, I said, "Here comes an honest man—a true son of Israel."

"How do you know about me?" Nathanael asked.

And I replied, "I could see you under the fig tree before Philip found you."

Nathanael replied, "Teacher, you are the Son of God—the King of Israel!"

I asked him, "Do you believe all this just because I told you I had seen you under the fig tree? You will see greater things than this."

Then I said, "The truth is, you will all see heaven open and the angels of God going up and down upon the Son of Man."

Jo. 1: 35-51

My First Miracle

Cana, in Galilee

The next day my mother was a guest at a wedding celebration in the village of Cana in Galilee.

My disciples and I were also invited to the celebration. The wine supply ran out during the festivities, so my mother spoke to me about the problem. "They have no more wine," she told me. "How does that concern you and me?" I asked. "My time has not yet come." But my mother told the servants, "Do whatever he tells you."

Six stone water pots were standing there; they were used for Jewish ceremonial purposes and held twenty to thirty gallons each. I told the servants, "Fill the jars with water." When the jars had been filled to the brim, I said, "Dip some out and take it to the master of ceremonies." So they followed my instructions.

When the master of ceremonies tasted the water that was now wine, not knowing where it had come from (though, of course, the servants knew), he called the bridegroom over. "Usually a host serves the best wine first," he said. "Then, when everyone is full and doesn't care, he brings out the less expensive wines. But you have kept the best until now!"

I was about thirty years old when I began my public ministry. This miraculous sign at Cana in Galilee was the first display of my glory. And my disciples believed in me.

After the wedding I went to Capernaum for a few days with my mother, my brothers, and my disciples.

Lu. 3:23a; Jo. 2:1-12

51

THE
FIRST OF
FOUR VISITS I MADE
TO JERUSALEM
DURING MY MINISTRY
SPRING, AD 27

THE
FIRST PASSOVER
(IN JERUSALEM)
SPRING, AD 27

I Cleared the Temple

It was time for the annual Passover celebration, and I went to Jerusalem.

In the Temple area I saw merchants selling cattle, sheep, and doves for sacrifices; and I saw money changers behind their counters. I made a whip from some ropes and chased them all out of the Temple. I drove out the sheep and oxen, scattered the money changers' coins over the floor, and turned over their tables.

Then, going over to the people who sold doves, I told them, "Get these things out of here. Don't turn my Father's house into a marketplace!" Then my disciples remembered this prophecy from the Scriptures:

Passion for God's house burns within me.

Ps. 69:9

"What right do you have to do these things?" the Jewish leaders demanded. "If you have this authority from God, show us a miraculous sign to prove it."

"All right," I replied. "Destroy this temple, and in three days I will raise it up."

"What!" they exclaimed. "It took forty-six years to build this Temple, and you can do it in three days?" But by "this temple," I meant my body.   3 1/2 YRS LATER

After I was raised from the dead, my disciples remembered that I had said this. And they believed both me and the Scriptures.

Because of the miraculous signs I did in Jerusalem at the Passover celebration, many people were convinced that I was indeed the Messiah. But I didn't trust them, because I know what people are really like. No one needed to tell me about human nature.

Jo. 2:13-25

My Meeting with Nicodemus

After dark one evening, a Jewish religious leader named Nicodemus, a Pharisee, came to speak with me. "Teacher," he said, "we all know that God sent you to teach us. Your miraculous signs are proof enough that God is with you."

I replied, "I assure you, unless you are born again, you can never see the Kingdom of God."

What do you mean?" exclaimed Nicodemus. "How can an old man go back into his mother's womb and be born again?"

57

I replied, "The truth is, no one can enter the Kingdom of God without being born of water and the Spirit. Humans can reproduce only human life, but the Holy Spirit gives new life from heaven. So don't be surprised at my statement that you must be born again. Just as you can hear the wind but can't tell where it comes from or where it is going, so you can't explain how people are born of the Spirit."

"What do you mean?" Nicodemus asked.

I replied, "You are a respected Jewish teacher, and yet you don't understand these things? I assure you, I am telling you what we know and have seen, and yet you won't believe us. But if you don't even believe me when I tell you about things that happen here on earth, how can you possibly believe if I tell you what is going on in heaven? For only I, the Son of Man, have come to earth and will return to heaven again. And as Moses lifted up the bronze snake on a pole in the wilderness, so I, the Son of Man, must be lifted up on a pole, so that everyone who believes in me will have eternal life.

"For God so loved the world that he gave his only Son, so that everyone who believes in him will not perish but have eternal life. God did not send his Son into the world to condemn it, but to save it.

"There is no judgment awaiting those who trust him. But those who do not trust him have already been judged for not believing in the only Son of God. Their judgment is based on this fact: The light from heaven came into the world, but they loved the darkness more than the light, for their actions were evil. They hate the light because they want to sin in the darkness. They stay away from the light for fear their sins will be exposed and they will be punished. But those who do what is right come to the light gladly, so everyone can see that they are doing what God wants."

Jo. 3:1-21

Rom 8:1

Again, My Cousin John Testified about Me

Aenon, in Judea

Afterward my disciples and I left Jerusalem, but we stayed in Judea for a while and baptized there.

At this time John the Baptist was baptizing at Aenon, near Salim, because there was plenty of water there and people kept coming to him for baptism. This was before John was put into prison. At that time a certain Jew began an argument with John's disciples over ceremonial cleansing. John's disciples came to him and said, "Teacher, the man you met on the other side of the Jordan River, the one you said was the Messiah, is also baptizing people. And everybody is going over there instead of coming here to us."

58

John replied, "God in heaven appoints each person's work. You yourselves know how plainly I told you that I am not the Messiah. I am here to prepare the way for him— that is all. The bride will go where the bridegroom is. A bridegroom's friend rejoices with him. I am the bridegroom's friend, and I am filled with joy at his success. He must become greater and greater, and I must become less and less.

"He has come from above and is greater than anyone else. I am of the earth, and my understanding is limited to the things of earth, but he has come from heaven. He tells what he has seen and heard, but how few believe what he tells them! Those who believe him discover that God is true. For he is sent by God. He speaks God's words, for God's Spirit is upon him without measure or limit. The Father loves his Son, and he has given him authority over everything. And all who believe in God's Son have eternal life. Those who don't obey the Son will never experience eternal life, but the wrath of God remains upon them."

Jo. 3:22-36

My Cousin John Was Imprisoned by Herod

Machaerus, in Perea

John had publicly criticized Herod Antipas, the king and ruler of Galilee, for marrying Herodias, his brother's wife, and for many other wrongs he had done. So Herod put John in prison, adding this sin to his many others.

Lu. 3:19-20

I
VISITED
SAMARIA

A Woman at Jacob's Well

AD 27 Sychar, in Samaria

I learned that the Pharisees had heard, "Jesus is baptizing and making more disciples than John" (though I myself didn't baptize them—my disciples did). Later on, when I heard that John had been arrested by Herod Antipas, I left Judea to return to Galilee.

I had to go through Samaria on the way.

Eventually I came to the Samaritan village of Sychar, near the parcel of ground that Jacob gave to his son Joseph. Jacob's well was there; and I, tired from the long walk, sat wearily beside the well about noontime. Soon a Samaritan woman came to draw water, and I said to her, "Please give me a drink." I was alone at the time because my disciples had gone into the village to buy some food.

The woman was surprised, for Jews refuse to have anything to do with Samaritans. She said to me, "You are a Jew, and I am a Samaritan woman. Why are you asking me for a drink?"

I replied, "If you only knew the gift God has for you and who I am, you would ask me, and I would give you living water."

"But sir, you don't have a rope or a bucket," she said, "and this is a very deep well. Where would you get this living water? And besides, are you greater than our ancestor Jacob who gave us this well? How can you offer better water than he and his sons and his cattle enjoyed?"

I replied, "People soon become thirsty again after drinking this water. But the water I give them takes away thirst altogether. It becomes a perpetual spring within them, giving them eternal life."

"Please, sir," the woman said, "give me some of that water! Then I'll never be thirsty again, and I won't have to come here to haul water."

"Go and get your husband," I told her.

"I don't have a husband," the woman replied.

I said, "You're right! You don't have a husband—for you have had five husbands, and you aren't even married to the man you're living with now."

"Sir," the woman said, "you must be a prophet. So tell me, why is it that you Jews insist that Jerusalem is the only place of worship, while we Samaritans claim it is here at Mount Gerizim, where our ancestors worshiped?"

I replied, "Believe me, the time is coming when it will no longer matter whether you worship the Father here or in Jerusalem. You Samaritans know so little about the one you worship, while we Jews worship that which we know, for salvation comes through the Jews. But the time is coming and is already here when true worshipers will

63

worship the Father in spirit and in truth. The Father is looking for anyone who will worship him that way. For God is Spirit, so those who worship him must worship in spirit and truth."

The woman said, "I know the Messiah will come—the one who is called Christ. When he comes, he will explain everything to us."

Then I told her, "I am the Messiah!"

Just then my disciples arrived. They were astonished to find me talking to a woman, but none of them asked me why I was doing it or what we had been discussing. The woman left her water jar beside the well and went back to the village and told everyone, "Come and meet a man who told me everything I ever did! Can this be the Messiah?" So the people came streaming from the village to see me.

Meanwhile, the disciples were urging me to eat. "No," I said, "I have food you don't know about." "Who brought it to him?" the disciples asked each other.

Then I explained: "My nourishment comes from doing the will of God, who sent me, and from finishing his work. Do you think the work of harvesting will not begin until the summer ends four months from now? Look around you! Vast fields are ripening all around us and are ready now for the harvest. The harvesters are paid good wages, and the fruit they harvest is people brought to eternal life. What joy awaits both the planter and the harvester alike! You know the saying, 'One person plants and someone else harvests.' And it's true. I sent you to harvest where you didn't plant. Others had already done the work, and you will gather the harvest."

Many Samaritans from the village believed in me because the woman had said, "He told me everything I ever did!" When they came out to see me, they begged me to stay at their village. So I stayed for two days, long enough for many of them to hear my message and believe. Then they said to the woman, "Now we believe because we have heard him ourselves, not just because of what you told us. He is indeed the Savior of the world."

Mt. 4:12; Mk. 1:14a; Jo. 4:1-42

I
MADE
MY HOME
IN
THE TOWN
OF CAPERNAUM

I Was Welcomed in Galilee

At the end of the two days' stay, I went on into Galilee filled with the Holy Spirit's power.

I had previously said, "A prophet is honored everywhere except in his own country"; therefore, instead of going to Nazareth, I went to Capernaum—a town beside the Sea of Galilee, in the region of Zebulun and Naphtali.

The Galileans welcomed me, for they had been in Jerusalem at the Passover celebration and had seen all my miraculous signs. This fulfilled Isaiah's prophecy:

> *In the land of Zebulun and of Naphtali, beside the sea, beyond the Jordan River—in Galilee where so many Gentiles live—the people who sat in darkness have seen a great light. And for those who lived in the land where death casts its shadow, a light has shined.*

Isa. 9:1-2

From then on, I began to preach God's Good News. "At last the time has come!" I announced. "The Kingdom of God is near! Turn from your sins and believe this Good News and turn to God because the Kingdom of Heaven is near."

Mt. 4:13-17; Mk. 1:14b-15; Lu. 4:14a, 31a; Jo. 4:43-45

I Healed a Nobleman's Son

Cana, in Galilee

In the course of my journey through Galilee, I arrived at the town of Cana, where I had turned the water into wine. There was a government official in the city of Capernaum whose son was very sick. When he heard that I had come from Judea and was traveling in Galilee, he went over to Cana.

He found me and begged me to come to Capernaum with him to heal his son, who was about to die. I asked, "Must I do miraculous signs and wonders before you people will believe in me?"

The official pleaded, "Lord, please come now before my little boy dies." Then I told him, "Go back home. Your son will live!" And the man believed my word and started home.

While he was on his way, some of his servants met him with the news that his son was alive and well. He asked them when the boy had begun to feel better, and they replied, "Yesterday afternoon at one o'clock his fever suddenly disappeared!" Then the father realized it was the same time that I had told him, "Your son will live."

And the officer and his entire household believed in me.

This was my second miraculous sign in Galilee after coming from Judea.

Jo. 4:46-54

PART III

THE
SECOND YEAR
OF MY
MINISTRY

AD 28

I Was Rejected in My Home Town

Early AD 28   Nazareth

Soon I became well-known throughout the surrounding country. I taught in their synagogues and was praised by everyone.

When I came to the village of Nazareth, my boyhood home, I went as usual to the synagogue on the Sabbath and stood up to read the Scriptures. The scroll containing the messages of Isaiah the prophet was handed to me, and I unrolled the scroll to the place where it says:

> *The Spirit of the Lord is upon me, for he has appointed me to preach Good News to the poor. He has sent me to proclaim that captives will be released, that the blind will see, that the downtrodden will be freed from their oppressors, and that the time of the Lord's favor has come.*

Isa. 61:1-2

I rolled up the scroll, handed it back to the attendant, and sat down. Everyone in the synagogue stared at me intently. Then I said, "This Scripture has come true today before your very eyes!"

All who were there spoke well of me and were amazed by the gracious words that fell from my lips. "How can this be?" they asked. "Isn't this Joseph's son?"

Then I said, "Probably you will quote me that proverb, 'Physician, heal yourself'—meaning 'Why don't you do miracles here in your hometown like those you did in Capernaum?' But the truth is, no prophet is accepted in his own hometown.

"Certainly there were many widows in Israel who needed help in Elijah's time, when there was no rain for three and a half years, and hunger stalked the land. Yet Elijah was not sent to any of them. He was sent instead to a widow of Zarephath—a foreigner in the land of Sidon. Or think of the prophet Elisha, who healed Naaman, a Syrian, rather than the many lepers in Israel who needed help."

When they heard this, the people in the synagogue were furious. Jumping up, they mobbed me and took me to the edge of the hill on which the city was built. They intended to push me over the cliff, but I slipped away through the crowd and left them.

Lu. 4:14b-30

I Called Fishermen to Fish for People

The shores of the Sea of Galilee

One day as I was walking along the shores of the Sea of Galilee, I saw two brothers—Simon, also called Peter, and Andrew* —fishing

71

with a net, for they were commercial fishermen. I called out to them, "Come, be my disciples, and I will show you how to fish for people!" And they left their nets at once and went with me.

A little farther up the shore I saw two other brothers, Zebedee's sons, James and John, sitting in a boat mending their nets. I called out to them to come, too, and they immediately followed me, leaving their father behind in the boat with the hired men.

Mt. 4:18-22; Mk. 1:16-20

News about Me Spread throughout the Land

I traveled throughout Galilee teaching in the synagogues, preaching everywhere the Good News about the Kingdom.

I healed people who had every kind of sickness and disease. News about me spread far beyond the borders of Galilee so that the sick were soon coming to be healed from as far away as Syria. And whatever their illness and pain, or if they were possessed by demons, or were epileptics, or were paralyzed—I healed them all, expelling demons from many people. Large crowds followed me wherever I went—people from Galilee, the Ten Towns, Jerusalem, from all over Judea, and from east of the Jordan River.

Mt. 4:23-25

MARKET Places spread
where News was
at

I

CAST OUT

DEMONS

AND

I

HEALED

THE SICK

⅓ of the
angels are
evil - were
CAST out of Heaven
with SATAN

I Cast Out Demons

Annotations in margin: Day of Rest; WORKERS of the Devil — WORKERS of Evil (spiritual)

Capernaum, in the synagogue

My companions and I went to the town of Capernaum, and every Sabbath day I went into the synagogue and taught the people. There too, they were amazed at my teaching for I taught as one who had real authority—quite unlike the teachers of religious law.

Once when I was in the synagogue, a man possessed by an evil spirit began shouting at me, "Go away! Why are you bothering us, Jesus of Nazareth? Have you come to destroy us? I know who you are—the Holy One sent from God!" I cut him short. "Be silent!" I told the demon. "Come out of the man!"

Annotation in margin: Demons destroy

At that, the evil spirit screamed and threw the man to the floor into a convulsion as the crowd watched; but then it left him without hurting him further.

Amazement gripped the audience, and they began to discuss what had happened. "What sort of new teaching is this?" they asked excitedly. "What authority and power this man's words possess! Even evil spirits obey his orders and flee at his command!" The news of what I had done spread quickly like wildfire throughout the entire area of Galilee.

Mk. 1:21-28; Lu. 4:31b, 31b-37

I Healed the Sick

Simon Peter's home

After leaving the synagogue that day, my disciples and I went over to Simon and Andrew's home, where I found Simon's mother-in-law very sick in bed with a high fever, and James and John were with them. They told me about her right away.

"Please heal her," everyone begged. I went to her bedside and standing there, I spoke to the fever, rebuking it, and touched her hand. As I took her by the hand and helped her to sit up, the fever suddenly left, and immediately her temperature returned to normal. Then she got up at once and prepared a meal for us.

As the sun went down that evening, people throughout the village brought sick family members and demon-possessed people to me. And I healed all the sick. No matter what their diseases were, the touch of my hand healed every one. This fulfilled the word of the Lord through Isaiah, who said,

He took our sicknesses and removed our diseases.

Isa. 53:4

75

And a huge crowd of people from all over Capernaum gathered outside the door to watch.

I healed great numbers of sick people who had many different kinds of diseases, and I ordered many demons to come out of their victims. All the spirits fled when I commanded them to leave. They came out shouting, "You are the Son of God." But because they knew I was the Messiah, I stopped them and told them to be silent and refused to allow them to speak.

The next morning I awoke long before daybreak and went alone into the wilderness to pray. Later Simon and the others went out to find me. They said, "Everyone is asking for you." But I replied, "We must go on to other towns as well and I will preach to them too, because that is why I came."

The crowds searched everywhere for me, and when they finally found me, they begged me not to leave them. But I replied, "I must preach the Good News of the Kingdom of God in other places, too, because that is why I was sent."

So I continued to travel around, throughout the region of Galilee and throughout Judea, teaching in the synagogues, expelling demons from many people.

Mt. 8:14-17; Mk. 1:29-39; Lu. 4:38-44

I Spoke of a Great Harvest

I traveled through all the cities and villages of that area, teaching in the synagogues and announcing the Good News about the Kingdom. And wherever I went, I healed people of every sort of disease and illness. I felt great pity for the crowds that came, because their problems were so great and they didn't know where to go for help. They were like sheep without a shepherd.

I said to my disciples, "The harvest is so great, but the workers are so few. So pray to the Lord who is in charge of the harvest; ask him to send out more workers for his fields."

Mt. 9:35-38

I Reminded My Disciples that They Would Fish for Men

The shores of the Sea of Galilee

One day as I was preaching on the shore of the Sea of Galilee, great crowds pressed in on me to listen to the word of God.

I noticed two empty boats at the water's edge, for the fishermen had left them and were washing their nets. Stepping into one of the boats, I asked Simon, its owner, to push it out into the water. So I sat in the boat and taught the crowds from there.

When I had finished speaking, I said to Simon, "Now go out where it is deeper and let down your nets, and you will catch many fish."

"Master," Simon replied, "we worked hard all last night and didn't catch a thing. But if you say so, we'll try again."

And this time their nets were so full they began to tear! A shout for help brought their partners in the other boat, and soon both boats were filled with fish and on the verge of sinking.

When Simon Peter realized what had happened, he fell to his knees before me and said, "Oh, Lord, please leave me—I'm too much of a sinner to be around you." For he was awestruck by the size of their catch, as were the others with him. His partners, James and John, the sons of Zebedee, were also amazed.

I replied to Simon, "Don't be afraid! From now on you will be fishing for people!" And as soon as they landed, they left everything and followed me.

Lu. 5:1-11

A Man with Leprosy Came to Me

In one of the villages, I met a man with an advanced case of leprosy.

The man with leprosy approached me. Suddenly, when he saw me, he fell to the ground, face down in the dust begging to be healed. "Lord," he said, "if you want to, you can make me well again." He knelt before me, worshiping.

Moved with pity, I reached out and touched the man. "I want to," I said. "Be healed!" And instantly the leprosy disappeared—the man was healed. Then I instructed him not to tell anyone what had happened. I sent him on his way and told him sternly, "Go right over to the priest and let him examine you. Don't talk to anyone along the way. Take along the offering required in the law of Moses for those who have been healed of leprosy, so everyone will have proof of your healing." Yet despite my instructions, as the man went on his way, he spread the news, telling everyone what had happened to him.

The report of my power spread even faster, and vast crowds came to hear me preach and to be healed of their diseases. As a result, such crowds soon surrounded me that I couldn't enter a town anywhere publicly. I had to stay out in the secluded places, and people from everywhere came to me there. But I often withdrew to the wilderness for prayer.

Mt 8:2-4; Mk 1:40-45; Lu 5:12-16

77

Four Men Brought Their Paralyzed Friend to Me

Several days later I climbed into a boat and went back across the lake to Capernaum, my own town, and the news of my arrival spread quickly through the town.

Soon the house where I was staying was so packed with visitors that there wasn't room for one more person, not even outside the door. And I preached the word to them. And my healing power was strongly with me.

One day while I was teaching, four men arrived carrying a paralyzed man on a sleeping mat. They tried to push through the crowd, but couldn't get to me; so they went up to the roof, took off some tiles, dug through the clay above my head, and lowered the sick man down into the crowd, still on his mat, right in front of me. Seeing their faith, I said to the paralyzed man, "Take heart, my son! Your sins are forgiven."

Some Pharisees and teachers of religious law were sitting nearby. (It seemed that these men showed up from every village in all Galilee and Judea, as well as from Jerusalem.) "Who does this man think he is?" the Pharisees and teachers of religious law said among themselves. "This is blasphemy! This man talks as if he is God! Who but God can forgive sins?"

I knew what they were thinking, so I asked them, "Why are you thinking such evil thoughts? Why do you think this is blasphemy? Is it easier to say to the paralyzed man, 'Your sins are forgiven' or 'Get up, pick up your mat, and walk'? I will prove that I, the Son of Man, have the authority on earth to forgive sins."

Then I turned to the paralyzed man and said, "Stand up, take up your mat, and go on home, because you are healed!"

And immediately, as everyone watched, the man jumped to his feet, picked up his mat, pushed his way through the stunned onlookers, and went home praising God. Everyone was gripped with great wonder and awe as they saw this happen right before their very eyes. "We've never seen anything like this before!" they exclaimed. And they praised God for sending a man with such great authority, saying over and over again, "We have seen amazing things today."

Mt. 9:1-8; Mk. 2:1-12; Lu. 5:17-26

I Chose a Tax Collector to Be My Disciple

Then I went out to the lakeshore again and taught the crowds that gathered around me. Later, walking down the road as I left the town, I saw Matthew,* son of Alphaeus, sitting at his tax collection booth. "Come be my disciple," I said to him. So Levi got up, left everything, and followed me.

That night Matthew held a banquet in his home with me as the guest of honor. Matthew invited my disciples and me to be his dinner guests, along with his fellow tax collectors and many other notorious sinners. (There were many people of this kind among the crowds that followed me.)

The Pharisees were indignant. When some of the teachers of religious law who were Pharisees saw me eating with people like that, they complained bitterly to my disciples, "Why does your teacher eat and drink with such scum?"

When I heard this, I answered them, "Healthy people don't need a doctor—sick people do." Then I added, "Now, go and learn the meaning of this Scripture:

I want you to be merciful; I don't want your sacrifices.

Hos. 6:6

"For I have come to call sinners to turn from their sins, not to spend my time with those who think they are already good enough."

Mt. 9:9-13; Mk. 2:13-17; Lu. 5:27-32

I Was Asked about Fasting

John the Baptist's disciples and the Pharisees sometimes fasted. The religious leaders complained that my disciples were feasting instead of fasting. "John the Baptist's disciples always fast and pray," they declared, "and so do the disciples of the Pharisees. Why are yours always feasting?" One day the disciples of John came to me and asked, "Why do we and the Pharisees fast, but your disciples don't fast?"

I responded, "Should wedding guests mourn—fast—while celebrating with the groom? Of course not. They cannot fast while they are with the groom. But someday he will be taken away from them, and then they will fast."

Then I gave them this illustration: "No one tears a piece of unshrunk cloth from a new garment and uses it to patch an old garment. The new garment would be torn, and the patch wouldn't even match the old garment. For the new patch shrinks and pulls away from the old cloth, leaving an even bigger hole than before. And no one puts new wine into old wineskins. The old wineskins would burst from the pressure, spilling the wine and ruining the skins. New wine must be stored in new wineskins. That way both the wine and the wineskins are preserved. But no one who drinks the old wine seems to want the fresh and the new. 'The old is better,' they say."

Mt. 9:14-17; Mk. 2:18-22; Lu. 5:33-39

MY
SECOND VISIT
TO JERUSALEM
SPRING, AD 28

THE
SECOND PASSOVER
(IN JERSALEM)
SPRING, AD 28

I Broke Sabbath Tradition

Sabbath created by God on 7th day — no day of rest *(handwritten)*

Afterward I returned to Jerusalem for one of the Jewish holy days.

Inside the city, near the Sheep Gate, was the pool of Bethesda, with five covered porches. Crowds of sick people—blind, lame, or paralyzed—lay on the porches. One of the men lying there had been sick for thirty-eight years. When I saw him and knew how long he had been ill, I asked him, "Would you like to get well?"

"I can't sir," the sick man said, "for I have no one to help me into the pool when the water is stirred up. While I am trying to get there, someone else always gets in ahead of me."

I told him, "Stand up, pick up your sleeping mat, and walk!"

Instantly, the man was healed! He rolled up the mat and began walking! But this miracle happened on the Sabbath day. So the Jewish leaders objected. They said to the man who was cured, "You can't work on the Sabbath! It's illegal to carry that sleeping mat!"

He replied, "The man who healed me said to me, 'Pick up your sleeping mat and walk.'"

"Who said such a thing as that?" they demanded. The man didn't know, for I had disappeared into the crowd.

Afterward I found him in the Temple and told him, "Now you are well; so stop sinning, or something even worse may happen to you." Then the man went to find the Jewish leaders and told them it was I who had healed him.   *rules more important than helping (handwritten)*

So the Jewish leaders began harassing me for breaking the Sabbath rules. But I replied, "My Father never stops working, so why should I?" So the Jewish leaders tried all the more to kill me. In addition to disobeying the Sabbath rules, I had spoken of God as my Father, thereby making myself equal with God.

I continued, saying, "I assure you, the Son can do nothing by himself. I do only what I see the Father doing. Whatever the Father does, the Son also does. For the Father loves the Son and tells him everything he is doing, and I will do far greater things than healing this man. You will be astonished at what I do. I will even raise from the dead anyone I want to, just as the Father does. And the Father leaves all judgment to me, so that everyone will honor me, just as they honor the Father. But if you refuse to honor me, then you are certainly not honoring the Father who sent me.

"I assure you, those who listen to my message and believe in God who sent me have eternal life. They will never be condemned for their sins, but they have already passed from death into life.

John 9 (handwritten)

"And I assure you that the time is coming, in fact it is here, when the dead will hear my voice—the voice of the Son of God. And those who listen will live. The Father has life in himself, and he has granted me to have life in myself. And he has given me authority to judge all mankind because I am the Son of Man.

"Don't be so surprised! Indeed, the time is coming when all the dead in their graves will hear the voice of God's Son, and they will rise again. Those who have done good will rise to eternal life, and those who have continued in evil will rise to judgment. But I do nothing without consulting the Father. I judge as I am told. And my judgment is absolutely just, because it is according to the will of God who sent me; it is not merely my own.

"If I were to testify on my own behalf, my testimony would not be valid. But someone else is also testifying about me, and I can assure you that everything he says about me is true. In fact, you sent messengers to listen to John the Baptist, and he preached the truth. But the best testimony about me is not from a man, though I have reminded you about John's testimony so you might be saved. John shone brightly for a while, and you benefited and rejoiced. But I have a greater witness than John—my teachings and my miracles. They have been assigned to me by the Father, and they testify that the Father has sent me. And the Father himself has also testified about me. You have never heard his voice or seen him face to face, and you do not have his message in your hearts, because you do not believe me—the one he sent to you.

"You search the Scriptures because you believe they give you eternal life. But the Scriptures point to me! Yet you refuse to come to me so that I can give you this eternal life.

"Your approval or disapproval means nothing to me, because I know you don't have God's love within you. For I have come to you representing my Father, and you refuse to welcome me, even though you readily accept others who represent only themselves. No wonder you can't believe! For you gladly honor each other, but you don't care about the honor that comes from God alone.

"Yet it is not I who will accuse you of this before the Father. Moses will accuse you! Yes, Moses, on whom you set your hopes. But if you had believed Moses, you would have believed me because he wrote about me. And since you don't believe what he wrote, how will you believe what I say?"

Jo. 5:1-47

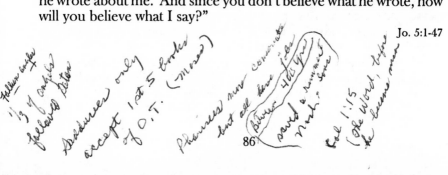

86

Sabbath
is down
sun down
Fri to sun
down sat.

Galilee

I Taught about the Sabbath

One Sabbath day I was walking through some grain fields. My disciples were hungry, so they began breaking off heads of wheat, rubbing off the husks in their hands, and eating the grain.

Some Pharisees saw them do it and protested, "Your disciples shouldn't be doing that! It's against the law to work by harvesting grain on the Sabbath."

But I replied to them, "Haven't you ever read in the Scriptures what King David did when he and his companions were hungry? He went into the house of God (during the days when Abiathar was high priest), ate the special bread reserved for the priests alone, and then gave some to his companions. That was breaking the law, too.

"And haven't you ever read in the law of Moses that the priests on duty in the Temple may work on the Sabbath? I tell you, there is one here who is even greater than the Temple! But you would not have condemned those who aren't guilty if you knew the meaning of the Scripture:

I want you to be merciful; I don't want your sacrifices.

Hos. 6:6

Then I said to them, "The Sabbath was made to benefit people, and not people to benefit the Sabbath. And I, the Son of Man, am master even of the Sabbath!"

On another Sabbath Day, I noticed a man with a deformed right hand in the synagogue while I was teaching. The Pharisees asked me, "Is it legal to work by healing on the Sabbath Day?" (They were, of course, hoping I would say yes, so they could bring legal charges against me.)

But I knew their thoughts. I said to the man with the deformed hand, "Come and stand here where everyone can see." So the man came forward. The teachers of the religious law and the Pharisees watched closely to see whether I would heal the man on the Sabbath. If I did, they planned to condemn me.

Then I turned to my critics and said, "I have a question for you. Is it legal to do good deeds on the Sabbath, or is it a day for doing harm? Is this a day to save a life or destroy it?" But they wouldn't answer me.

I looked around at them angrily, because I was deeply disturbed by their hard hearts and asked, "If you had one sheep, and it fell into a well on the Sabbath, wouldn't you get to work and pull it out? Of course you would. And how much more valuable is a person than a sheep! Yes, it is right to do good on the Sabbath."

I looked around at them one by one and then I said to the man, "Reach out your hand." The man reached out his hand, and it became normal again, just like the other one!

At this, my enemies were wild with rage and began to discuss what to do with me. Then the Pharisees went away and called a meeting with the supporters of Herod to discuss plans for killing me.

But I knew what they were planning. I left the area, and many people followed me.

✝ Mt. 12:1-15; Mk. 2:23-3:6; Lu. 6:1-11

HOW
I CAME
TO CHOOSE
THE
TWELVE

I Chose the Twelve

Summer, AD 28   *Near Capernaum*

One day soon afterward I went to a mountain to pray, and I prayed to God all night. At daybreak I called together all of my disciples, and they came to me. Then I chose twelve of them to be my regular companions, calling them apostles. I sent them out to preach, and I gave them authority to cast out evil spirits and to heal every kind of disease and illness. Here are the names of the twelve I chose:

first Simon (I also called him Peter), *Cephas (Rock)*
then Andrew (Peter's brother),
James and John (the sons of Zebedee, but I nicknamed them "Sons of Thunder"),
Philip,
Bartholomew,*
Matthew (the tax collector), *Levi*
Thomas,
James (son of Alphaeus),
Thaddaeus** (son of James),
Simon (the Zealot),
Judas Iscariot (who later betrayed me).

Mt. 10:1b-4; Mk. 3:13-19; Lu. 6: 12-16

People Came from Everywhere

When we came down the slopes of the mountain to the lake, my disciples stood with me on a large, level area, surrounded by many of my followers and by the crowds.

There were people from all over Galilee, Judea, Jerusalem, Idumea, from east of the Jordan River, and even as far north as the seacoasts of Tyre and Sidon. The news about my miracles had spread far and wide, and vast numbers of people had come to see me for themselves. They had come to hear me and to be healed. I instructed my disciples to bring around a boat and to have it ready in case I was crowded off the beach.

There had been many healings that day. Many sick people were crowding around me, trying to touch me because healing power went out from me. As a result, they were all cured.

And I cast out many evil spirits.

Whenever those possessed by evil spirits caught sight of me, they would fall down in front of me shrieking, "You are the Son of God!" But I strictly warned them not to say who I was. This fulfilled the prophecy of Isaiah concerning me:

Look at my Servant, whom I have chosen. He is my Beloved, and I am very pleased with him. I will put my Spirit upon him, and he will proclaim justice to the nations. He will not fight or shout; he will not raise his voice in public. He will not crush those who are weak, or quench the smallest hope, until he brings full justice with his final victory. And his name will be the hope of the world.

Isa. 42:1-4

Mt. 12:16-21; Mk. 3:7-12; Lu. 6: 17-19

THOUSANDS GATHERED ON A MOUNTAINSIDE TO HEAR ME

The Beatitudes

Summer, AD 28　　*A hill near Capernaum*

One day as the crowds were gathering, I went up to the mountainside with my disciples and sat down to teach them. I turned to my disciples and said,

"God blesses those who realize their need for him, for the Kingdom of Heaven is given to them. God blesses those who mourn, for they will be comforted. God blesses those who weep now, for the time will come when they will laugh with joy. God blesses those who are gentle and lowly, for the whole earth will belong to them. God blesses those who are hungry and thirsty for justice, for they will receive it in full. God blesses those who are merciful, for they will be shown mercy. God blesses those whose hearts are pure, for they will see God. God blesses those who work for peace, for they will be called the children of God. God blesses those who are persecuted because they live for God, for the Kingdom of Heaven is theirs.

"God blesses you who are hated and excluded and cursed because you are identified with me, the Son of Man. God blesses you when you are mocked and persecuted and lied about because you are my followers. When that happens, rejoice! Be happy about it! Be very glad! Yes, leap for joy! For a great reward awaits you in heaven. And remember, the ancient prophets were also treated that way by your ancestors.

"What sorrows await you who are rich, for you have your only happiness now. What sorrows await you who are satisfied and prosperous now, for a time of awful hunger is before you. What sorrows await you who laugh carelessly, for your laughing will turn to sorrow. What sorrows await you who are praised by the crowds, for their ancestors also praised false prophets."

Mt. 5:1-12; Lu. 6:20-26

I Taught about the Kingdom

"You are the salt of the earth. But what good is salt if it has lost its flavor? Can you make it useful again? It will be thrown out and trampled underfoot as worthless. You are the light of the world—like a city on a mountain, glowing in the night for all to see. Do not hide your light under a basket! Instead, put it on a stand and let it shine for all. In the same way, let your good deeds shine out for all to see, so that everyone will praise your heavenly Father.

"Do not misunderstand why I have come. I did not come to abolish the law of Moses or the writings of the prophets. No, I came

94

to fulfill them. I assure you, until heaven and earth disappear, even the smallest detail of God's law will remain until its purpose is achieved. So if you break the smallest commandment and teach others to do the same, you will be the least in the Kingdom of Heaven. But anyone who obeys God's laws and teaches them will be great in the Kingdom of Heaven.

"But I warn you—unless you obey God better than the teachers of religious law and the Pharisees do, you cannot enter the Kingdom of Heaven at all!

"You have heard that the law of Moses says,

Do not murder. If you commit murder, you are subject to judgment.

Exodus 20:13; Deut. 5:17

But I say, if you are angry with someone, you are subject to judgment! If you say to your friend, 'You idiot,' you are in danger of being brought before the court. And if you curse someone, you are in danger of the fires of hell.

"So if you are standing before the altar in the Temple, offering a sacrifice to God, and you suddenly remember that someone has something against you, leave your sacrifice there beside the altar. Go and be reconciled to that person. Then come and offer your sacrifice to God. Come to terms quickly with your enemy before it is too late and you are dragged into court, handed over to an officer, and thrown in jail. I assure you that you won't be free again until you have paid the last penny.

"You have heard that the law of Moses says,

Do not commit adultery.

Exodus 20:14; Deut. 5:18

But I say, anyone who even looks at a woman with lust in his eye has already committed adultery with her in his heart. So if your eye— even if it is your good eye—causes you to lust, gouge it out and throw it away. It is better for you to lose one part of your body than for your whole body to be thrown into hell. And if your hand causes you to sin, cut it off and throw it away. It is better for you to lose one part of your body than for your whole body to be thrown into hell.

"You have heard that the law of Moses says,

A man can divorce his wife by merely giving her a letter of divorce.

Deut. 24:1

But I say that a man who divorces his wife, unless she has been unfaithful, causes her to commit adultery. And anyone who marries a divorced woman commits adultery.

"Again, you have heard that the law of Moses says,

Do not break your vows; you must carry out the vows you have made to the Lord.

Num. 30:2

But I say, don't take any vows! If you say, 'By heaven!' it is a sacred vow because heaven is God's throne. And if you say, 'By earth!' it is a sacred vow because the earth is his footstool. And don't swear 'By Jerusalem!' for Jerusalem is the city of the great King. Do not even swear 'By my head!' for you can't turn one hair white or black. Just say a simple 'Yes, I will,' or 'No, I won't.' Your word is enough. To strengthen your promise with a vow shows that something is wrong.

"You have heard that the law of Moses says,

If an eye is injured, injure the eye of the person who did it. If a tooth gets knocked out, knock out the tooth of the person who did it.

Exodus 21:24; Lev. 24:20; Deut. 19:21

But I say, don't resist an evil person! If you are slapped on the right cheek, turn the other, too.

"If someone demands your shirt, offer you coat also. If a soldier demands that you carry his gear a mile, carry it two miles. Do not turn away from those who want to borrow. Give what you have to anyone who asks you for it; and when things are taken away from you, don't try to get them back. Do for others as you would like them to do for you.

"Do you think you deserve credit merely for loving those who love you? Even the sinners do that! And if you do good only to those who do good to you, is that so wonderful? Even sinners do that much! And if you lend money only to those who can repay you, what good is that? Even sinners will lend to their own kind for a full return.

"You have heard that the law of Moses says,

Love your neighbor

Lev. 19:18

and hate your enemy. But I say, love your enemies! Do good to those who hate you. Pray for the happiness of those who curse you. Pray for those who hurt you. Pray for those who persecute you! Do good to them! Lend to them! And don't be concerned that they might not repay.

"Then your reward from heaven will be great, and you will be acting as true children of the Most High, for he is kind to the unthankful and to those who are wicked. Your Father in heaven gives his sunlight to both the evil and the good, and he sends rain on the just and the unjust, too. You must be compassionate, just as your Father is compassionate. If you love only those who love you,

96

what good is that? Even corrupt tax collectors do that much. If you are kind only to your friends, how are you different from anyone else? Even pagans do that. But you are to be perfect, even as your Father in heaven is perfect.

"Take care! Do not do your good deeds publicly, to be admired, because then you will lose the reward from your Father in heaven. When you give a gift to someone in need, don't shout about it as the hypocrites do—blowing trumpets in the synagogues and streets to call attention to their acts of charity! I assure you, they have received all the reward they will ever get. But when you give to someone, don't tell your left hand what your right hand is doing. Give your gifts in secret, and your Father, who knows all secrets, will reward you."

Mt. 5:13-6:4; Lu. 6:27-36

I Taught about Prayer and Fasting

"And now about prayer. When you pray, don't be like the hypocrites who love to pray publicly on street corners and in the synagogues where everyone can see them. I assure you, that is all the reward they will ever get. But when you pray, go away by yourself, shut the door behind you, and pray to your Father secretly. Then your Father, who knows all secrets, will reward you.

"When you pray, don't babble on and on as people of other religions do. They think their prayers are answered only by repeating their words again and again. Don't be like them, because your Father knows exactly what you need even before you ask him! Pray like this:

"Our Father in heaven, may your name be honored. May your kingdom come soon. May your will be done here on earth, just as it is in heaven. Give us our food for today, and forgive us our sins, just as we have forgiven those who have sinned against us. And don't let us yield to temptation, but deliver us from the evil one.

"If you forgive those who sin against you, your heavenly Father will forgive you. But if you refuse to forgive others, your Father will not forgive your sins.

"And when you fast, don't make it obvious, as the hypocrites do, who try to look pale and disheveled so people will admire them for their fasting. I assure you, that is the only reward they will ever get. But when you fast, comb your hair and wash your face. Then no one will suspect you are fasting, except your Father, who knows what you do in secret. And your Father who knows all secrets will reward you.

"Do not store up treasures here on earth, where they can be eaten by moths and get rusty, and where thieves break in and steal.

Store your treasures in heaven, where they will never become moth-eaten or rusty and where they will be safe from thieves. Wherever your treasure is, there your heart and thoughts will also be.

"Your eye is a lamp for your body. A pure eye lets sunshine into your soul. But an evil eye shuts out the light and plunges you into darkness. If the light you think you have is really darkness, how deep that darkness will be!

"No one can serve two masters. For you will hate one and love the other, or be devoted to one and despise the other. You cannot serve both God and money."

Mt. 6:5-24

The Cares of Life

"So I tell you, don't worry about everyday life—whether you have enough food, drink, and clothes. Doesn't life consist of more than food and clothing? Look at the birds. They don't need to plant or harvest or put food in barns because your heavenly Father feeds them. And you are far more valuable to him than they are. Can all your worries add a single moment to your life? Of course not.

"And why worry about your clothes? Look at the lilies and how they grow. They don't work or make their clothing, yet Solomon in all his glory was not dressed as beautifully as they are. And if God cares so wonderfully for flowers that are here today and gone tomorrow, won't he more surely care for you? You have so little faith!

"So don't worry about having enough food or drink or clothing. Why be like the pagans who are so deeply concerned about these things? Your heavenly Father already knows all your needs, and he will give you all you need from day to day if you live for him and make the Kingdom of God your primary concern.

"So don't worry about tomorrow, for tomorrow will bring its own worries. Today's trouble is enough for today.

"Stop judging others, and you will not be judged. Whatever measure you use in judging others, it will be used to measure how you are judged. Stop criticizing others, or it will all come back on you. If you forgive others, you will be forgiven. For others will treat you as you treat them. *

"If you give you will receive. Your gift will return to you in full measure, pressed down, shaken together to make room for more, and running over. Whatever measure you use in giving—large or small—it will be used to measure what is given back to you."

Then I gave the following illustration:

"What good is it for one blind person to lead another? The first one will fall into a ditch and pull the other down also. A student is

98

not greater than the teacher. But the student who works hard* will become like the teacher.

"And why worry about the speck in your friend's eye when you have a log in your own? How can you think of saying, 'Friend, let me help you get rid of that speck in your eye,' when you can't see past the log in your own eye? Hypocrite! First get rid of the log from your own eye; then perhaps you will see well enough to deal with the speck in your friend's eye.

"Don't give what is holy to unholy people. Don't give pearls to swine! They will trample the pearls, then turn and attack you."

Mt. 6:25-7:6; Lu. 6:37-42

Ask, Look, Knock

"Keep on asking, and you will be given what you ask for. Keep on looking, and you will find. Keep on knocking, and the door will be opened. For everyone who asks, receives. Everyone who seeks, finds. And the door is opened to everyone who knocks. You parents—if your children ask for a loaf of bread, do you give them a stone instead? Or if they ask for a fish, do you give them a snake? Of course not! If you sinful people know how to give good gifts to your children, how much more will your heavenly Father give good gifts to those who ask him.

"Do for others what you would like them to do for you. This is a summary of all that is taught in the law and the prophets.

"You can enter God's Kingdom only through the narrow gate. The highway to hell is broad, and its gate is wide for the many who choose the easy way. But the gateway to life is small, and the road is narrow, and only a few ever find it.

"Beware of false prophets who come disguised as harmless sheep, but are really wolves that will tear you apart. You can detect them by the way they act, just as you can identify a tree by its fruit. You don't pick grapes from thornbushes, or figs from thistles. A healthy tree produces good fruit, and an unhealthy tree produces bad fruit. So every tree that does not produce good fruit is chopped down and thrown into the fire. Yes, the way to identify a tree or a person is by the kind of fruit that is produced. A good person produces good deeds from a good heart, and an evil person produces evil deeds from an evil heart. Whatever is in your heart determines what you say.

"Not all people who sound religious are really godly. They may refer to me as Lord, but they still won't enter the Kingdom of Heaven. The decisive issue is whether they obey my Father in heaven. On judgment day many will tell me, 'Lord, Lord, we prophesied in your name and cast out demons in your name and performed many miracles in your name.' But I will reply, 'I never knew you. Go away. Why do you call me Lord, when you won't obey me?'

"I will show you what it's like when someone comes to me, listens to my teaching, and then obeys me. It is like a person who builds a house on a strong foundation laid upon the underlying solid rock. When the rain comes in torrents and the floodwaters rise and the winds beat against the house, it won't collapse; it stands firm because it is well built on rock. But anyone who hears my teaching and doesn't obey it is foolish, like a person who builds a house on sand without a foundation. When the rains and floods come and the winds beat down against that house, it will fall with a mighty crash and crumble into a heap of ruins."

After I finished speaking, the crowds were amazed at my teaching, for I taught as one who had real authority—quite unlike the teachers of religious law.

Mt. 7:7-29; Lu. 6:-43-49

I Met a Man with True Faith

Capernaum

Large crowds followed me as I came down the mountainside. When I had finished saying all this, I went back to Capernaum.

Now the highly valued slave of a Roman officer was sick and near death. When the officer heard about me, he sent some respected Jewish leaders to ask me to come and heal his slave. So they earnestly begged me to come with them and help the man. "If anyone deserves your help, it is he," they said, "for he loves the Jews and even built a synagogue for us."

So I went with them. Just before we arrived at the house, the officer came and pleaded with me, "Lord, my young servant lies in bed paralyzed and racked with pain."

I said, "I will come and heal him."

Then the officer said, "Lord, don't trouble yourself by coming to my home, for I am not worthy of such an honor. Just say the word from where you are, and my servant will be healed. I know because I am under the authority of my superior officers, and I have authority over my soldiers. I only need to say, 'Go,' and they go, or 'Come,' and they come. And if I say to my slaves, 'Do this or that,' they do it."

When I heard this, I was amazed. Turning to the crowd, I said, "I tell you, I haven't seen faith like this in all the land of Israel!

"And I tell you this, that many Gentiles will come from all over the world and sit down with Abraham, Isaac, and Jacob at the feast in the Kingdom of Heaven. But many Israelites—those for whom the Kingdom was prepared—will be cast into outer darkness, where there will be weeping and gnashing of teeth."

Then I said to the Roman officer, "Go on home. What you have believed has happened." The young servant was healed that same hour. And when the officer's friends returned to his house, they found the slave completely healed.

Mt. 8:1, 5-13; Lu. 7:1-10

I Raised a Child from the Dead

Nain, in Galilee

Soon afterward I went with my disciples to the village of Nain, with a great crowd following me.

A funeral procession was coming out as I approached the village gate.

The boy who had died was the only son of a widow, and many mourners from the village were with her. When I saw her, my heart overflowed with compassion.

"Don't cry!" I said. Then I walked over to the coffin and touched it, and the bearers stopped. "Young man," I said, "get up." Then the dead boy sat up and began to talk to those around him! And I gave him back to his mother.

Great fear swept the crowd, and they praised God, saying, "A mighty prophet has risen among us" and "We have seen the hand of God at work today." The report of what I had done that day spread all over Judea and even out across its borders.

Lu. 7:11-17

I Testified Concerning John the Baptist

Galilee

The disciples of John the Baptist, who was now in prison, told John about everything I was doing. So John called for two of his disciples and he sent them to ask me, "Are you really the Messiah we've been expecting, or should we keep looking for someone else?"

John's two disciples found me and said to me, "John the Baptist sent us to ask, 'Are you really the Messiah we've been expecting, or should we keep looking for someone else?'"

At that time I cured many people of their various diseases, and I cast out evil spirits and restored sight to the blind. Then I told John's disciples, "Go back to John and tell him what you have seen and heard—the blind see, the lame walk, the lepers are cured, the deaf hear, the dead are raised to life, and the Good News is being preached

101

to the poor. And tell him, 'God blesses those who are not offended by me.'"

After they left, I talked to the crowds about John. "Who is this man in the wilderness that you went out to see? Did you find him weak, as a reed moved by every breath of wind? Or were you expecting to see a man dressed in expensive clothes? No, people who wear beautiful clothes and live in luxury are found in palaces, not in the wilderness. Were you looking for a prophet? Yes, and he is more than a prophet. John is the man to whom the Scriptures refer when they say,

Look, I am sending my messenger before you, and he will prepare your way before you.

Mal. 3:1

"I assure you, of all who have ever lived, none is greater than John the Baptist. Yet even the most insignificant person in the Kingdom of God is greater than he is! And from the time John the Baptist began preaching and baptizing until now, the Kingdom of Heaven has been forcefully advancing, and violent people attack it. For before John came, all the teachings of the Scriptures looked forward to this present time. And if you are willing to accept what I say, he is Elijah, the one the prophets said would come. Anyone who is willing to hear should listen and understand."

When they heard this, all the people, including the unjust tax collectors, agreed that God's plan was right, for they had been baptized by John.

But the Pharisees and experts in religious law rejected God's plan for them, for they had refused John's baptism.

"How shall I describe this generation?" I asked. "With what will I compare them? They are like a group of children playing a game in the public square. They complain to their friends, 'We played wedding songs, and you weren't happy, so we played funeral songs, but you weren't sad.' For John the Baptist didn't drink wine and he often fasted, and you say, 'He's demon possessed.' And I, the Son of Man, feast and drink, and you say, 'He's a glutton and a drunkard, and a friend of the worst sort of sinners!' But wisdom is shown to be right by what results from it, by the lives of those who follow it."

Mt. 11:2-19; Lu. 7:18-35

I Was Anointed with Perfume and Tears

One of the Pharisees asked me to come to his home for a meal, so I accepted the invitation and sat down to eat. A certain immoral woman heard I was there and brought a beautiful jar filled with expensive perfume. Then she knelt behind me at my feet, weeping. Her tears fell on my feet, and she wiped them off with her hair. Then she kept kissing my feet and putting perfume on them.

When the Pharisee who was the host saw what was happening and who the woman was, he said to himself, "This proves that Jesus is no prophet. If God had really sent him, he would know what kind of woman is touching him. She's a sinner!"

Then I spoke up and answered his thoughts. "Simon," I said to the Pharisee, "I have something to say to you."

"All right, Teacher," Simon replied, "go ahead."

Then I told him a story: "A man loaned money to two people— five hundred pieces of silver to one and fifty pieces to the other. But neither of them could repay him, so he kindly forgave them both, canceling their debts. Who do you suppose loved him more after that?"

Simon answered, "I suppose the one for whom he canceled the larger debt."

"That's right," I said. Then I turned to the woman and said to Simon, "Look at this woman kneeling here. When I entered your home, you didn't offer me water to wash the dust from my feet, but she has washed them with her tears and wiped them with her hair. You didn't give me a kiss of greeting, but she has kissed my feet again and again from the time I first came in. You neglected the courtesy of olive oil to anoint my head, but she has anointed my feet with rare perfume. I tell you, her sins—and they are many—have been forgiven, so she has shown me much love. But a person who is forgiven little shows only little love."

Then I said to the woman, "Your sins are forgiven."

The men at the table said among themselves, "Who does this man think he is, going around forgiving sins?"

And I said to the woman, "Your faith has saved you; go in peace."

Lu. 7:36-50

Several Women Joined Me as I Traveled

Not long afterward I began a tour of the nearby cities and villages to announce the Good News concerning the Kingdom of God. I took my twelve disciples with me, along with some women I had healed and from whom I had cast out evil spirits. Among them were Mary Magdalene, from whom I had cast out seven demons; Joanna, the wife of Chuza, Herod's business manager; Susanna; and many others who were contributing from their own resources to support my disciples and me.

Lu. 8:1-3

I Was Accused of Being Possessed by Satan

Late Summer, AD 28   *On the western shore of the Sea of Galilee*

When I returned to the house where I was staying, the crowds began to gather again, and soon my disciples and I couldn't even find time to eat. When my family heard what was happening, they tried to take me home with them. "He's out of his mind," they said.

Then a demon-possessed man, who was both blind and unable to talk, was brought to me. I healed the man so that he could both speak and see.

The crowd was amazed. "Could it be that Jesus is the Messiah, the Son of David?" they wondered out loud.

But when the Pharisees and the teachers of religious law who had arrived from Jerusalem heard about the miracle, they said, "He's possessed by Satan. No wonder he can cast out demons. He gets his power from Satan, the prince of demons."

I knew their thoughts and replied, "How can Satan cast out Satan? Any kingdom at war with itself will collapse. A city or home divided against itself is doomed. You say I am empowered by the prince of demons. But if Satan is fighting against himself by empowering me to cast out his demons, how can he stand? He will never survive. His own kingdom will not survive. And if I am empowered by the prince of demons, what about your own followers? They cast out demons, too, so they will judge you for what you have said.

"But if I am casting out demons by the Spirit of God, then the Kingdom of God has arrived among you. Let me illustrate this. You can't enter a strong man's house and rob him without first tying him up. Only then can his house be robbed! For when Satan, who is completely armed, guards his palace, it is safe—until someone who is stronger attacks and overpowers him, strips him of his weapons, and carries off his belongings.

"Anyone who isn't helping me opposes me, and anyone who isn't working with me is actually working against me.

"I assure you that any sin can be forgiven, including blasphemy, but anyone who blasphemes against the Holy Spirit will never be forgiven. Anyone who blasphemes against me, the Son of Man, can be forgiven, but blasphemy against the Holy Spirit will never be forgiven, either in this world or the world to come. It is an eternal sin." I told them this because they were saying I had an evil spirit.

I said to them by way of illustration, "A tree is identified by its fruit. Make a tree good, and its fruit will be good. Make a tree bad, and its fruit will be bad. You brood of snakes! How could evil men like you speak what is good and right? For whatever is in your heart determines what you say. A good person produces good words from a good heart, and an evil person produces evil words from an evil heart. And I tell you this, that you must give an account on judgment day of every idle word you speak. The words you say now reflect your fate then; either you will be justified by them or you will be condemned.

"No one lights a lamp and then hides it or puts it under a basket. Instead, it is put on a lampstand to give light to all who enter the room. Your eye is a lamp for your body. A pure eye lets sunshine into your soul. But an evil eye shuts out the light and plunges you into darkness. Make sure that the light you think you have is not really darkness. If you are filled with light, with no dark corners, then your whole life will be radiant, as though a floodlight is shining on you."   *I Cor 4:3-4*

your mind is
an eye to the
body

Mt. 12:22-37; Mk. 3:20-30; Lu. 11:14-15, 17-23, 33-36

I Denounced the Hypocrisy of the Pharisees

As I was speaking, one of the Pharisees invited me home for a meal. So I went in and took my place at the table.

My host was amazed to see that I sat down to eat without first performing the ceremonial washing required by Jewish custom. Then I said to him, "You Pharisees are so careful to clean the outside of the cup and the dish, but inside you are still filthy—full of greed and wickedness! Fools! Didn't God make the inside as well as the outside? So give to the needy what you greedily possess, and you will be clean all over.

"But how terrible it will be for you Pharisees! For you are careful to tithe even the tiniest part of your income, but you completely forget about justice and the love of God. You should tithe, yes, but you should not leave undone the more important things.

"How terrible it will be for you Pharisees! For how you love the seats of honor in the synagogues and the respectful greetings from everyone as you walk through the markets! Yes, how terrible it will be for you. For you are like hidden graves in a field. People walk over them without knowing the corruption they are stepping on."

"Teacher," said an expert in religious law, "you have insulted us, too, in what you just said."

"Yes," I said, "how terrible it will be for you experts in religious law! For you crush people beneath impossible religious demands, and you never lift a finger to help ease the burden. How terrible it will be for you! For you build tombs for the very prophets your ancestors killed long ago. Murderers! You agree with your ancestors that what they did was right. You would have done the same yourselves. This is what God in his wisdom said about you: 'I will send prophets and apostles to them, and they will kill some and persecute the others.'

"And you of this generation will be held responsible for the murder of all God's prophets from the creation of the world—from the murder of Abel to the murder of Zechariah, who was killed between the altar and the sanctuary. Yes, it will surely be charged against you.

"How terrible it will be for you experts in religious law! For you hide the key to knowledge from the people. You don't enter the Kingdom yourselves, and you prevent others from entering."

As I finished speaking, the Pharisees and teachers of religious law were furious. From that time on they grilled me with many hostile questions, trying to trap me into saying something they could use against me.

Lu. 11:37-54

They Wanted a Sign

One day some teachers of religious law and Pharisees came to test me.

Others asked for a miraculous sign and said, "Teacher, we want you to show us a miraculous sign to prove that you are from God."

As the crowd pressed in on me, I replied, "These are evil times, and this evil, faithless generation keeps asking me to show them a miraculous sign. But the only sign I will give them is the sign of the prophet Jonah.

"What happened to him was a sign to the people of Nineveh that God had sent him. What happens to me will be a sign that God has sent me, the Son of Man, to these people. For as Jonah was in the belly of the great fish for three days and three nights, so I, the Son of Man, will be in the heart of the earth for three days and three nights. The people of Nineveh will rise up against this generation on judgment day and condemn it, because they repented at the preaching of Jonah. And now someone greater than Jonah is here—and you refuse to repent.

"The queen of Sheba will also rise up against this generation on judgment day and condemn it, because she came from a distant land to hear the wisdom of Solomon. And now someone greater than Solomon is here—and you refuse to listen to him.

"When an evil spirit leaves a person, it goes into the desert, seeking rest but finding none. Then it says, 'I will return to the person I came from.' So it returns and finds its former home empty, swept, and clean. Then the spirit finds seven other spirits more evil than itself, and they all enter the person and live there. And so that person is worse off than before. That will be the experience of this evil generation."

As I was speaking, a woman in the crowd called out, "God bless your mother—the womb from which you came, and the breasts that nursed you!"

I replied, "But even more blessed are all who hear the word of God and put it into practice."

Then I asked them, "Would anyone light a lamp and then put it under a basket or under a bed to shut out the light? Of course not! No one would light a lamp and then cover it up or put it under a bed. No, lamps are mounted in the open on a stand, where the light will shine and they can be seen by those entering the house. For everything that is hidden or secret will eventually be brought to light and made plain to all.

"Anyone who is willing to hear should listen and understand! And be sure to pay attention to what you hear. The more you do this, the more you will understand—and even more besides.

"To those who are open to my teaching, more understanding will be given. But to those who are not listening, even what they think they have will be taken away from them."

As I was speaking to the crowd, my mother and brothers arrived at the house where I was teaching. They couldn't get to me because of the crowd, so they stood outside and sent word for me to come out and talk with them.

Mt. 12:38-46; Mk. 3:31-32a, 4:21-25; Lu. 8:16-19, 11:16, 24-32

My True Family

Someone told me, "Your mother and brothers and sisters* are outside, and they want to speak to you." I replied, "Who is my mother? Who are my brothers? My mother and my brothers are all those who hear the message of God and obey it."

Then I pointed to my disciples and looked at those around me. "These are my mother and brothers. Anyone who does the will of my Father in heaven is my brother and sister and mother!"

Mt. 12:47-50; Mk. 3:32b-35; Lu. 8:20-21

107

I
TAUGHT
WITH PARABLES

I Told Simple Stories

Then I said, "Here is another illustration of what the Kingdom of God is like:

"A farmer planted seeds in a field, and then he went on with his other activities. As the days went by, the seeds sprouted and grew without the farmer's help, because the earth produces crops on its own. First a leaf blade pushes through, then heads of wheat are formed, and finally the grain ripens. And as soon as the grain is ready, the farmer comes and harvests it with a sickle."

Here is another story I told:

"The Kingdom of Heaven is like a farmer who planted good seed in his field. But that night as everyone slept, his enemy came and planted weeds among the wheat. When the crop began to grow and produce grain, the weeds also grew. The farmer's servants came and told him, 'Sir, the field where you planted that good seed is full of weeds!'

"'An enemy has done it!' the farmer exclaimed.

"'Shall we pull out the weeds?' they asked.

"He replied, 'No, you'll hurt the wheat if you do. Let both grow together until the harvest. Then you will tell the harvesters to sort out the weeds and burn them and to put the wheat in the barns."

I asked, "How can I describe the Kingdom of God? What story should I use to illustrate it? The Kingdom of Heaven is like a tiny mustard seed planted in a field. Though this one is the smallest of seeds, it becomes the largest of garden plants and grows into a tree with long branches where birds can come and find shelter in its branches."

I always used many such stories and illustrations to teach the people as much as they were able to understand. In fact, in my public teaching, I never spoke to the crowds without using such parables; but afterward when I was alone with my disciples, I explained the meaning of them. This fulfilled the prophecy that said,

> *I will speak to you in parables; I will explain mysteries*
> *hidden since the creation of the world.*

Ps. 78:2

Leaving the crowds outside, I went into the house. Later, when I was alone with theTwelve, my disciples said, "Please explain the story of the weeds in the field."

"All right," I said, "I, the Son of Man, am the farmer who plants good seed. The field is the world, and the good seed represent the people of the Kingdom. The weeds are the people who belong to the evil one. The enemy who planted the weeds among the wheat is people of the Kingdom. The weeds are the people who belong to the evil one. The enemy who planted the weeds among the wheat is the devil. The harvest is the end of the world, and the harvesters are the angels.

"Just as the weeds are separated out and burned, so it will be at the end of the world. I, the Son of Man, will send my angels, and they will remove from my Kingdom everything that causes sin and all who do evil, and they will throw them into the furnace and burn them. There will be weeping and gnashing of teeth. Then the godly will shine like the sun in their Father's Kingdom. Anyone who is willing to hear should listen and understand!

"The Kingdom of Heaven is like a treasure that a man discovered hidden in a field. In his excitement, he hid it again and sold everything he owned to get enough money to buy the field—and to get the treasure, too!

"Again, the Kingdom of Heaven is like a pearl merchant on the lookout for choice pearls. When he discovered a pearl of great value, he sold everything he owned and bought it!

"Again, the Kingdom of Heaven is like a fishing net that is thrown into the water and gathers fish of every kind. When the net is full, they drag it up onto the shore, sit down, sort the good fish into crates and throw the bad ones away. That is the way it will be at the end of the world. The angels will come and separate the wicked people from the godly, throwing the wicked into the fire. There will be weeping and gnashing of teeth. Do you understand?"

"Yes," they said, "we do."

Then I added, "Every teacher of religious law who has become a disciple in the Kingdom of Heaven is like a person who brings out of the storehouse the new teachings as well as the old."*

Mt. 13:24-52; Mk. 4:10a, 26-34

The Farmer, the Seed, and the Soil

Later that same day, I left the house and went down to the lakeshore, where an immense crowd soon gathered from many towns to hear me. There was such a large crowd that I got into a boat and sat down and spoke from there as the people listened on the shore. I began to teach the people by telling many stories such as this one:

"Listen! A farmer went out to plant some seed. As he scattered it across his field, some seed fell on a footpath, and the birds came and ate it. Other seed fell on shallow soil with underlying rock. The plant sprang up quickly, but it soon wilted for lack of moisture beneath the hot sun, and died because the roots had no nourishment in the shallow soil. Other seed fell among thorns that shot up and choked out the tender blades so that it produced no grain. But some seed fell on fertile soil and produced a crop that was thirty, sixty, and even a hundred times as much as had been planted." When I had said this, I called out, "Anyone who is willing to hear should listen and understand!"

My disciples came with some others who were gathered around and asked me, "Why do you always tell stories when you talk to people? What do your stories mean?"

Then I explained to them, "I am using these stories to conceal everything about it from outsiders. You have been permitted to understand the secrets* of the Kingdom of Heaven, but others have not. To those who are open to my teaching, more understanding will be given, and they will have an abundance of knowledge. But to those who are not listening, even what they have will be taken away from them.** That is why I tell these stories, because people see what I do, but they don't really see. They hear what I say, but they don't really hear, and they don't understand. This fulfills the prophecy of Isaiah, which says:

> *You will hear my words, but you will not understand; you will see what I do, but you will not perceive its meaning. For the hearts of these people are hardened, and their ears cannot hear, and they have closed their eyes—so their eyes cannot see, and their ears cannot hear, and their hearts cannot understand, and they cannot turn to me and let me heal them.*

Isa. 6:9-10

"But blessed are your eyes, because they see; and your ears, because they hear. I assure you, many prophets and godly people have longed to see and hear what you have seen and heard, but they could not. But if you can't understand this story, how will you understand all the others I am going to tell?

"Now here is the explanation of the story I told you about the farmer sowing grain: The farmer I talked about is the one who brings God's message to others; the seed is God's message. The seed that fell on the hard path represents those who hear the Good News about the Kingdom and don't understand it. Then Satan comes at once and snatches the seed away from their hearts and prevents them from believing and being saved. The rocky soil represents those who hear the message and receive it with joy. But like young plants in such soil, their roots don't go very deep. At first they get along fine; they believe for awhile, but they wilt as soon as the hot winds of testing blow, when they have problems or are persecuted because they believe the Word. The thorny ground represents those who hear and accept the Good News, but all too quickly the message is

113

crowded out by the cares and pleasures of this life and the lure of wealth. And so they never grow to maturity. But the good soil represents honest, good-hearted people who hear God's message, cling to it,* and steadily produce a huge harvest—thirty, sixty, or even a hundred times as much as had been planted."

Mt. 13:1-23; Mk. 4:1-9, 10b-20; Lu. 8:4-15

I
CONTINUED
TO WORK
MIRACLES

I Calmed the Wind and Sea

Late AD 28

I noticed how large the crowds were growing. As evening came, I said to my disciples, "Let's cross to the other side of the lake. I was already in the boat, so they got in the boat and started out, leaving the crowds behind (although other boats followed). On the way across, I lay down for a nap, and while I was sleeping the wind began to rise. Suddenly a fierce storm came up that threatened to swamp us. High waves began to break into the boat until it was nearly full of water, and we were in danger.

I was sleeping at the back of the boat with my head on a cushion. Frantically the disciples woke me up, shouting, "Lord, save us! We're going to drown! Don't you even care?"

When I woke up, I rebuked the wind and said to the water, "Quiet down!" Suddenly the storm stopped and all was calm!

Then I asked them, "Where is your faith? Why are you so afraid? Do you still not have faith in me?" And the disciples just sat there filled with awe and amazement. "Who is this?" they asked themselves. "Even the wind and the waves obey him!"

Mt. 8:18, 23-27; Mk. 4:35-41; Lu. 8:22-25

I Healed a Demon-Possessed Man

Gergesa, on the eastern shore of the Sea of Galilee

So we arrived at the other side of the lake, in the land of the Gerasenes,* across the lake from Galilee.

Just as I was climbing out from the boat, a man possessed by demons came out to meet me. Homeless and naked, he had lived in a cemetery for a long time.

He lived among the tombs and could not be restrained, even with a chain. Whenever he was put into chains and shackles—as he often was—he snapped the chains from his wrists and smashed the shackles. No one was strong enough to control him. All day long and throughout the night, he would wander among the tombs and in the hills, screaming and hitting himself with stones.

When I was still some distance away, the man saw me. He ran to meet me and fell down before me. He gave a terrible scream, shrieking, "Why are you bothering us, Jesus, Son of the Most High God? Please, I beg you, for God's sake, don't torture us! You have no right to torture us before God's appointed time." For I had already commanded the spirit, "Come out of the man, you evil spirit." This spirit had often taken complete control of the man. Even

Even when he was shackled with the chains, he simply broke them and rushed out into the wilderness, completely under the demon's power.

"What is your name?" I asked.

"Legion," he replied, "because there are many of us here inside this man."

Then the spirits begged me again and again not to send them into the bottomless pit. There happened to be a large herd of pigs feeding on the hillside nearby. "If you cast us out, send us into that herd of pigs," the evil spirits begged. I gave them permission. "All right, go!" I commanded. So the evil spirits came out of the man and entered the pigs, and the entire herd of two thousand pigs plunged down the steep hillside into the lake, where they drowned.

When the herdsmen saw it, they fled to the nearby city and the surrounding countryside, telling everyone what had happened to the demon-possessed man as they ran.

The entire town came to meet me. A crowd soon gathered around me, for they wanted to see for themselves what had happened. But they were frightened when they saw the man who had been demon possessed, for he was sitting there quietly at my feet, fully clothed and perfectly sane. Those who had seen what had happened to the man and to the pigs told the others how the demon-possessed man had been healed.

And all the people in that region began pleading with me to go away and leave them alone, for a great wave of fear swept over them.

So I returned to the boat and left, crossing back to the other side. The man who had been demon-possessed begged to go, too. But I said, "No, go back to your friends, your family, and tell them all the wonderful things God has done for you and how merciful he has been."

So the man started off to visit the Ten Towns of that region and began to tell everyone about the great things I had done for him; and everyone was amazed at what he told them.

Mt. 8:28-34; Mk. 5:1-20; Lu. 8:26-39

I Healed the Sick and Raised the Dead
The western shore of the Sea of Galilee

When I went back across to the other side of the lake, a large crowd gathered around me on the shore and received me with open arms because they had been waiting for me. And now a man named Jairus, a leader of the local synagogue, came and fell down before me, begging me to come home with him. His only child was dying, a little girl twelve years old. "She is about to die," he said in desperation. "Please come and place your hands on her; heal her so she can live."

The disciples and I went with him, and the crowd thronged behind. And there was a woman in the crowd who had had a hemorrhage for twelve years. She had suffered a great deal from many doctors through the years and had spent everything she had to pay them, but she had gotten no better. In fact, she was worse. She had heard about me, so she came up behind me through the crowd and touched the fringe of my robe. For she thought to herself, "If I can just touch his clothing, I will be healed." Immediately the bleeding stopped, and she could feel that she had been healed!

I realized at once that healing power had gone out from me, so I turned around in the crowd and asked, "Who touched me?"

Everyone denied it, and Peter said, "Master, this whole crowd is pressing up against you. How can you ask, 'Who touched me?'"

But I kept looking around to see who had done it. I told him, "No, someone deliberately touched me, for I felt healing power go out from me." When the frightened woman realized that I knew, she began to tremble and fell to her knees at my feet and told me what she had done.

The whole crowd heard her explain why she had touched me and that she had immediately been healed. "Daughter, be encouraged!" I said to her, "Your faith has made you well. Go in peace. You have been healed."

While I was still speaking to her, messengers arrived from Jairus's home with the message, "Your little girl is dead. There is no use troubling the Teacher now." The leader of the synagogue came and knelt down before me. "My daughter has just died," he said, "but you can bring her back to life again if you just come and lay your hand upon her."

When I heard what had happened, I said to Jairus, "Do not be afraid. Just trust me, and she will be all right."

Then I stopped the crowd and wouldn't let anyone go with me except Peter and James and John. When we came to the home of the synagogue leader, I saw the commotion and heard the weeping and wailing and the funeral music. I went inside and spoke to the people. "Why all this weeping and commotion?" I asked. "Stop the weeping!" I said. "The child isn't dead; she is only asleep." The crowd laughed at me because they knew she had died, but I told them all to go outside. When the crowd was finally outside, I took Peter, James, John and the girl's father and mother into the room where the girl was lying. I took her by the hand and said in a loud voice, "Get up, my child!" And at that moment her life returned, and she immediately stood up and walked around! Then I told them to give her something to eat. Her parents were absolutely

119

overwhelmed. I commanded them not to tell anyone what had happened, but the report of the miracle swept through the entire countryside.

Mt. 9:18-26; Mk. 5:21-43; Lu. 8:40-56

The Blind Saw and the Mute Spoke

After I left the girl's home, two blind men followed along behind me, shouting, "Son of David, have mercy on us!" They went right into the house where I was staying, and I asked them, "Do you believe I can make you see?"

"Yes, Lord," they told me, "we do."

Then I touched their eyes and said, "Because of your faith, it will happen." And suddenly they could see! I sternly warned them, "Don't tell anyone about this." But instead, they spread my fame all over the region.

When they left, some people brought to me a man who couldn't speak because he was possessed by a demon. So I cast out the demon, and instantly the man could talk. The crowds marveled. "Nothing like this has ever happened in Israel!" they exclaimed.

But the Pharisees said, "He can cast out demons because he is empowered by the prince of demons."

Mt. 9:27-34

I Sent Out the Twelve

Late AD 28   Throughout Israel

Then I went out from village to village, teaching. One day I called together my twelve apostles and sent them out two by two, with authority to cast out evil spirits and to heal all diseases. I sent them out to tell everyone about the coming of the Kingdom of God and to heal the sick.

I sent the Twelve out with these instructions: "Don't go to the Gentiles or the Samaritans, but only to the people of Israel—God's lost sheep. Go and announce to them that the Kingdom of Heaven is near. Heal the sick, raise the dead, cure those with leprosy, and cast out demons. Give as freely as you have received!

"Don't take any food nor money with you. Don't carry a traveler's bag with extra sandals. Not even an extra coat. Don't even take a walking stick. Don't hesitate to accept hospitality, because those who work deserve to be fed. Be a guest in only one home. Whenever you enter a city or village search for a worthy man and stay in his home until you leave for the next town. When you are invited into someone's home, give it your blessing. If it turns out to be a worthy

120

home, let your blessing stand; if not, take back the blessing. If a village doesn't welcome you or listen to you, shake off the dust of that place from your feet as you leave. It is a sign that you have abandoned that village to its fate. I assure you, the wicked cities of Sodom and Gomorrah will be better off on the judgment day than that place will be.

"Look, I am sending you out as sheep among the wolves. Be as wary as snakes and harmless as doves. But beware! For you will be handed over to the courts and beaten in the synagogues. And you must stand trial before governors and kings because you are my followers. This will be your opportunity to tell them about me—yes, to witness to the world. When you are arrested, don't worry about what to say in your defense, because you will be given the right words at the right time. For it won't be you doing the talking—it will be the Spirit of your Father speaking through you.

"Brother will betray brother to death, fathers will betray their own children, and children will rise up against their parents and cause them to be killed. Everyone will hate you because of your allegiance to me. But those who endure to the end will be saved. When you are persecuted in one town, flee to the next. I assure you that I, the Son of Man, will return before you have reached all the towns of Israel.

"A student is not greater than the teacher. A servant is not greater than the master. The student shares the teacher's fate. The servant shares the master's fate. And since I, the master of the household, have been called the prince of demons, how much more will it happen to you, the members of the household! But don't be afraid of those who threaten you. For the time is coming when everything will be revealed; all that is secret will be made public. What I tell you now in the darkness, shout abroad when daybreak comes. What I whisper in your ears, shout from the housetops for all to hear!

"Don't be afraid of those who want to kill you. They can only kill your body; they cannot touch your soul. Fear only God, who can destroy both soul and body in hell. Not even a sparrow, worth only half a penny, can fall to the ground without your Father knowing it. And the very hairs on your head are all numbered. So don't be afraid; you are more valuable to him than a whole flock of sparrows.

"If anyone acknowledges me publicly here on earth, I will openly acknowledge that person before my Father in heaven. But if anyone denies me here on earth, I will deny that person before my Father in heaven.

"Don't imagine that I came to bring peace to the earth! No, I came to bring a sword. I have come to set a man against his father, and a daughter against her mother, and a daughter-in-law against her mother-in-law. Your enemies will be right in your own household!

If you love your father or mother more than you love me, you are not worthy of being mine; or if you love your son or daughter more than me, you are not worthy of being mine. If you refuse to take up your cross and follow me, you are not worthy of being mine. If you cling to your life, you will lose it; but if you give it up for me, you will find it.

"Anyone who welcomes you is welcoming me, and anyone who welcomes me is welcoming the Father who sent me. If you welcome a prophet as one who speaks for God, you will receive the same reward a prophet gets. And if you welcome good and godly people because of their godliness, you will be given a reward like theirs. And if you give even a cup of cold water to one of the least of my followers, you will surely be rewarded."

When I had finished giving these instructions to my twelve disciples, I went off teaching and preaching in towns throughout the country. So the disciples began their circuit of the villages, preaching the Good News and telling all they met to turn from their sins. And they cast out many demons and healed many sick people, anointing them with olive oil.

Mt. 10:1a, 5-11:1; Mk. 6:6b-13; Lu. 9:1-6

PART IV

THE
THIRD YEAR
OF MY
MINISTRY

AD 29

The Death of John the Baptist

Herod Antipas soon heard about me, because people everywhere were talking about me. Some were saying, "This must be John the Baptist come back to life again. That is why he can do miracles." Others were saying, "It is Elijah risen from the dead." Still others thought I was a prophet like the other great prophets of the past.

When Herod heard about me, he said to his advisers, "I beheaded John, so who is this man about whom I hear such stories?" And he tried to see me. When reports of my miracles reached Herod, he was worried and puzzled. He said, "John, the man I beheaded, has come back from the dead. That is why he can do such miracles."

Herod respected John, knowing that he was a good and holy man. But Herod was disturbed whenever he talked with John; even so, he liked to listen to him.

John kept telling Herod, "It's illegal for you to marry your brother's wife."

Herodias had been his brother Philip's wife, but Herod had married her. Herod had sent soldiers to arrest and imprison John as a favor to Herodias, for she was enraged and wanted John killed in revenge; but without Herod's approval she was powerless. Herod would have executed John, but he was afraid of a riot, because all the people believed John was a prophet, so he kept him under his protection.

But Herodias's chance finally came. It was Herod's birthday, and he gave a party for his palace aides, army officers, and the leading citizens of Galilee. Herodias' daughter performed a dance that greatly pleased them all. "Ask me for anything you like," the king said to the girl, "and I will give it to you." Then he promised with an oath, "I will give you whatever you ask, up to half of my kingdom!"

She went out and asked her mother, "What should I ask for?" Her mother told her, "Ask for the head of John the Baptist." At her mother's urging, the girl asked, "I want the head of John the Baptist, right now, on a tray!"

The king was sorry, but he was embarrassed to break his oath in front of his guests. So he issued the necessary orders and sent an executioner to the prison to cut off John's head and bring it to him. The soldier beheaded John in the prison, brought his head on a tray, and gave it to the girl, who took it over to her mother.

When John's disciples heard what had happened, they came for his body and buried him in a tomb. Then they told me what had happened. As soon as I heard the news, I went off by myself in a boat to a remote area to be alone.

Mt. 14:1-13a; Mk. 6:14-29; Lu. 9:7-9

THE
THIRD PASSOVER
(IN BETHSAIDA)
SPRING, AD 29

The Miracle of the Loaves and Fish

It was nearly time for the annual Passover celebration.

When the apostles returned to me from their ministry tour, they told me all they had done and what they had taught. Then I said, "Let's get away from the crowds for a while and rest. There were so many people coming and going that my apostles and I didn't even have time to eat. We left for a quieter spot by boat and crossed over the Sea of Galilee, also known as the Sea of Tiberias, toward the town of Bethsaida.

But many people saw us leaving. The crowds found out where I was going and followed by land. People from many towns and villages ran ahead along the shore and met us when we landed. A vast crowd was there as I stepped from the boat. I had compassion on them because they were like sheep without a shepherd. And so I welcomed them, teaching them all about the Kingdom of God and curing those who were ill.

Then I went up into the hills and sat down with my disciples around me. And I soon saw a great crowd of people climbing the hill, looking for me. A huge crowd kept following me wherever I went, because they saw my miracles as I healed the sick.

Late in the afternoon the twelve disciples came to me and said, "This is a desolate place and it is getting late. Send the crowds away to nearby villages and farms, so they can find food and lodging for the night. There is nothing to eat here in this deserted place."

But I said to them, "That isn't necessary—you feed them."

"Impossible! With what?" they asked. "It would take a small fortune to buy food for all this crowd!"

"How much food do you have?" I asked. "Go and find out."

Turning to Philip, I asked, "Philip, where can we buy bread to feed all these people?" I was testing Philip, for I already knew what I was going to do. Philip replied, "It would take a small fortune to feed them!"

Then Andrew, Simon Peter's brother, spoke up. "There's a young boy here with five barley loaves and two fish. But what good is that? Or are you expecting us to go and buy enough food for this huge crowd?" For there were about five thousand men there.

"Bring them here," I said.

Then I told the crowd to sit down in groups on the green grass. So they all sat down on the grassy slopes in groups of fifty or a hundred. Then I took the five loaves and two fish, looked up toward heaven, gave thanks to God, and asked God's blessing on the food. Breaking the loaves into pieces, I kept giving the bread and the fish to the disciples to give to the people. They all ate as much as they wanted until they were full.

"Now gather the leftovers," I told my disciples, "so that nothing is wasted." There were only five barley loaves to start with, but twelve baskets were filled with the leftover pieces of bread and fish the people did not eat! About five thousand men had eaten from those five loaves, in addition to all the women and children!

When the people saw this miraculous sign, they exclaimed, "Surely, he is the Prophet we have been expecting!" I saw that they were ready to take me by force and make me king, so I sent the people home.

Afterward I went higher up into the hills by myself to pray. Night fell while I was there alone. My disciples went down to the shore to wait for me. But as darkness fell and I still hadn't come back, they got into the boat and headed out across the open lake.

Mt. 14:13b-23; Mk. 6:30-46; Lu. 9:10-17; Jo. 6:1-17a

Peter and I Walked on Water

The Sea of Galilee

During the night, the disciples were in their boat out in the middle of the lake, and I was alone on land. A strong gale had risen and swept down upon them as they rowed, and the sea grew very rough with heavy waves. I saw that they were in serious trouble, rowing hard and struggling against the wind and fighting the waves. About three o'clock in the morning I came to them.

They were about three or four miles out when suddenly they saw me walking on the water toward the boat. The disciples were terrified when they saw me. I started to go past them, but they screamed in terror, thinking I was a ghost. So I called out to them at once. "It's all right," I said. "I am here. Don't be afraid." Then Peter called to me, "Lord, if it's really you, tell me to come to you by walking on the water."

"All right, come," I said.

So Peter went over the side of the boat and walked on the water toward me. But when he looked around at the high waves, he was terrified and began to sink. "Save me, Lord!" He shouted. Instantly I reached out my hand and grabbed him. "You don't have much faith," I said. "Why did you doubt me?"

They were eager to let me into the boat, and when we climbed back in, the wind stopped and immediately the boat arrived at our destination.

They were astonished by what they saw. Then the disciples worshiped me. "You really are the Son of God!" they exclaimed.

But they still didn't understand the miracle of the multiplied loaves, for their hearts were hard and they did not believe.

After we had crossed the lake, we arrived at Gennasaret. We anchored the boat and climbed out. The news of our arrival spread quickly. The people standing there recognized me at once, and they ran throughout the whole area and began carrying sick people to me on mats to be healed. Wherever I went—in villages and cities and out on the farms—they laid the sick in the market plazas and streets. The sick begged me to let them at least touch even the fringe of my robe, and all who touched it were healed.

That evening, we got into the boat and headed out across the lake toward Capernaum.

Mt. 14:24-36; Mk. 6:47-56; Jo. 6:17b-21

I Am the Bread of Life

At the synagogue in Capernaum

The next morning, back across the lake, crowds began gathering on the shore, waiting to see me. For they knew that my disciples and I had come over together and that my disciples had gone off in their boat, leaving me behind. Several boats from Tiberias landed near the place where I had blessed the bread and the people had eaten. When the crowd saw that I wasn't there, nor my disciples, they got into the boats and went across to Capernaum to look for me. When they arrived and found me, they asked, "Teacher, how did you get here?"

I replied, "The truth is, you want to be with me because I fed you, not because you saw the miraculous sign. But you shouldn't be so concerned about perishable things like food. Spend your energy seeking the eternal life that I, the Son of Man, can give you. For God the Father has sent me for that very purpose."

They replied, "What does God want us to do?"

I told them, "This is what God wants you to do: Believe in the one he has sent."

They replied, "You must show us a miraculous sign if you want us to believe in you. What will you do for us? After all, our ancestors ate manna while they journeyed through the wilderness! As the Scriptures say,

God gave them bread from heaven to eat.

Exodus 16:4; Ps. 78:24

I said, "I assure you, Moses didn't give them bread from heaven. My Father did. And now he offers you the true bread from heaven.

The true bread of God is the one who comes down from heaven and gives life to the world."

"Sir," they said, "give us that bread every day of our lives."

I replied, "I am the bread of life. No one who comes to me will ever be hungry again. Those who believe in me will never thirst. But you haven't believed in me even though you have seen me. However, those the Father has given me will come to me, and I will never reject them. For I have come down from heaven to do the will of God who sent me, not to do what I want. And this is the will of God, that I should not lose even one of all those he has given me, but that I should raise them to eternal life at the last day. For it is my Father's will that all who see his Son and believe in him should have eternal life—that I should raise them at the last day."

Then the people began to murmur in disagreement because I had said, "I am the bread from heaven." They said, "This is Jesus, the Son of Joseph. We know his father and mother. How can he say, 'I came down from heaven'?"

But I replied, "Don't complain about what I said. For people can't come to me unless the Father who sent me draws them to me, and at the last day I will raise them from the dead. As it is written in the Scriptures,

> *They will all be taught by God.*

Isa. 54:13

Everyone who hears and learns from the Father comes to me. (Not that anyone has ever seen the Father; only I, who was sent from God, have seen him.)

"I assure you, anyone who believes in me already has eternal life. Yes, I am the bread of life! Your ancestors ate manna in the wilderness, but they all died. However, the bread from heaven gives eternal life to everyone who eats it. I am the living bread that came down out of heaven. Anyone who eats this bread will live forever; this bread is my flesh, offered so the world may live."

Then the people began arguing with each other about what I meant. "How can this man give us his flesh to eat?" they asked.

So I said again, "I assure you, unless you eat the flesh of the Son of Man and drink his blood, you cannot have eternal life within you. But those who eat my flesh and drink my blood have eternal life, and I will raise them at the last day. For my flesh is the true food, and my blood is the true drink. All who eat my flesh and drink my blood remain in me, and I in them. I live by the power of the living Father who sent me; in the same way, those who partake of me will live because of me. I am the true bread from heaven. Anyone who eats this bread will live forever and not die as your ancestors did, even though they ate the manna."

I said these things while I was teaching in the synagogue in Capernaum.

Even my disciples said, "This is very hard to understand. How can anyone accept it?"

I knew within myself that my disciples were complaining, so I said to them, "Does this offend you? Then what will you think if you see me, the Son of Man, return to heaven again? It is the Spirit who gives eternal life. Human effort accomplishes nothing. And the very words I have spoken to you are spirit and life. But some of you don't believe me." (For I knew from the beginning who didn't believe, and I knew who would betray me.) Then I said, "That is what I meant when I said that people can't come to me unless the Father brings them to me."

At this point many of my disciples turned away and deserted me. Then I turned to the Twelve and asked, "Are you going to leave, too?"

Simon Peter replied, "Lord, to whom would we go? You alone have the words that give eternal life. We believe them, and we know you are the Holy One of God."

Then I said, "I chose the twelve of you, but one is a devil." I was speaking of Judas, son of Simon Iscariot, one of the Twelve, who would betray me.

After this I stayed in Galilee, going from village to village. I wanted to stay out of Judea where the Jewish leaders were plotting my death.

Jo. 6:22-7:1

Jewish Tradition *vs* Inner Purity

Spring, AD 29

One day some Pharisees and teachers of religious law arrived from Jerusalem to confront me.

They noticed that some of my disciples failed to follow the usual Jewish ritual of hand washing before eating. (The Jews, especially the Pharisees, do not eat until they have poured water over their cupped hands, as required by their ancient traditions. Similarly, they eat nothing bought from the market unless they have immersed their hands in water. This is but one of many traditions they have clung to—such as their ceremony of washing cups, pitchers, and kettles.)

"Why do your disciples disobey our age-old traditions?" they demanded. "They ignore our tradition of ceremonial hand washing before they eat."

133

I replied, "Why do you, by your traditions, violate the direct commandments of God? You reject God's laws in order to hold on to your own traditions. For instance, Moses gave you this law from God:

Honor your father and mother,

Exodus 20:12; Deut. 5:16

and

Anyone who speaks evil of father or mother must be put to death.

Exodus 21:17; Lev. 20:9

But you say, 'You don't need to honor your parents by caring for their needs if you give the money to God instead.' You say, 'It is all right for people to say to their parents, 'Sorry, I can't help you, for I have vowed to give God what I could have given to you.' You let them disregard their needy parents. As such, you break the law of God in order to protect your own tradition. And this is only one example. There are many, many others. By your own tradition you nullify the direct commandment of God.

"You hypocrites! Isaiah was prophesying about you when he said,

These people honor me with their lips, but their hearts are far away. Their worship is a farce, for they replace God's commands with their own man-made teaching.

Isa.9:13

For you ignore God's specific laws and substitute your own traditions."

Then I called to the crowds to come and hear. "All of you listen to what I say and try to understand. You are not defiled by what you eat; you are defiled by what you say and do!" I said.

Then I went into the house to get away from the crowds, and my disciples came to me and asked, "Do you realize you offended the Pharisees by what you said?"

I replied, "Every plant not planted by my heavenly Father will be rooted up, so ignore them. They are blind guides leading the blind, and if one blind person guides another, they will both fall into a ditch."

Then Peter asked me, "Explain what you meant when you said people aren't defiled by what they eat."

"Don't you understand, either?" I asked him. "Can't you see that what you eat won't defile you? Anything you eat passes through the stomach and then goes out the body." (By saying this, I showed that every kind of food is acceptable.) Food doesn't come in contact with your heart. Evil words come from an evil heart and defile the person who says them.

And then I added, "Evil thoughts defile you. For from the heart come evil thoughts, murder, adultery, greed, wickedness, deceit, envy, pride, foolishness, theft, lying, slander, eagerness for lustful pleasure, and all other sexual immorality. All these vile things come from within; they are what defile you and make you unacceptable to God. Eating with unwashed hands could never defile you and make you unacceptable to God!"

Mt. 15:1-20; Mk. 7:1-23

I
TRAVELED
WIDELY

The Faith of a Gentile Woman

AD 29 The coastal region of Tyre

Then I left Galilee and went north to the region of Tyre. I tried to keep it secret that I was there, but I couldn't. As usual, news of my arrival spread fast. A Gentile woman whose little girl was possessed by an evil spirit had heard about me, and right away she came to me pleading, "Have mercy on me, O Lord, Son of David! For my daughter has a demon in her, and it is severely tormenting her."

She fell at my feet and begged me to release her child from the demon's control. But I gave her no reply—not even a word.

Then my disciples urged me to send her away. "Tell her to leave," they said. "She is bothering us with her begging."

Since she was a Gentile, born in Syrian Phoenicia, I told her, "I was sent only to help the people of Israel—God's lost sheep—not the Gentiles.

But she worshiped me and pleaded again, "Lord, help me!"

Then I said to the woman, "First I should help my own family, the Jews.* It isn't right to take food from the children and throw it to the dogs."

She replied, "Yes, Lord, that's true. But even the dogs are permitted to eat some crumbs that fall beneath the master's table from the children's plates.

"Good answer," I said. "Woman," I said to her, "your faith is great. And because you have answered so well, your request is granted. I have healed your daughter."

And when she arrived home, her little girl was lying quietly in bed, and the demon was gone.

Mt. 15:21-28; Mk. 7:24-30

I Healed the Deaf and Mute

Region of the Ten Towns

I left Tyre and went to Sidon, then back to the Sea of Galilee and the region of the Ten Towns. A deaf man with a speech impediment was brought to me, and the people begged me to lay my hands on the man to heal him. I led him to a private place away from the crowd. I put my fingers into the man's ears. Then, spitting onto my own fingers, I touched the man's tongue with the spittle. And looking up to heaven, I sighed and commanded, "Be opened!" Instantly the man could hear perfectly and speak plainly!

I told the crowd not to tell anyone, but the more I told them not to, the more they spread the news. Again and again they said, "Everything he does is wonderful. He even heals those who are deaf and mute."

Mk. 7:31-37

I Again Miraculously Fed Thousands

Summer, AD 29   Southeastern shores of the Sea of Galilee

I climbed a hill and sat down near the Sea of Galilee. A vast crowd brought me the lame, blind, crippled, mute, and many others with physical difficulties, and they laid them before me. And I healed them all. The crowd was completely amazed! Those who hadn't been able to speak were talking, the crippled were made well, the lame were walking around, and those who had been blind could see again! And they praised the God of Israel.

And about this time, the people ran out of food again. I called my disciples and told them, "I feel sorry for these people. They have been here with me for three days, and they have nothing left to eat. And if I send them home without feeding them, they will faint along the road. For some of them have come a long distance."

The disciples asked, "And where are we supposed to find enough food for all of them to eat out here in the wilderness?"

"How many loaves of bread do you have?" I asked.

"Seven," they replied, "and a few small fish."

So I told all the people to sit down on the ground. Then I took the seven loaves and the fish, thanked God for them, broke them into pieces, and gave them to the disciples, who distributed the food to the crowd.

They all ate until they were full, and when the scraps were picked up, there were seven large baskets of food left over!

There were about four thousand men who were fed that day, in addition to all the women and children. Then I sent the people home after they had eaten.

Immediately after this, I got into a boat with my disciples and crossed over to the region of Dalmanutha.*

Mt. 15:29-37; Mk. 8:1-10

The Yeast of the Pharisees and Sadducees

Dalmanutha, in Galilee

When the Pharisees and Sadducees heard that I had arrived, they came to argue with me. Testing me to see if I was from God,

140

they demanded, "Give us a miraculous sign from heaven to prove yourself."

When I heard this, I sighed deeply and said, "Why do you people keep demanding a miraculous sign? I assure you, I will not give this generation any such sign.

"You know the saying, 'Red sky at night means fair weather tomorrow, red sky in the morning means foul weather all day.' You are good at reading the weather signs in the sky, but you can't read the obvious signs of the times! Only an evil, faithless generation would ask for a miraculous sign, but the only sign I will give is the sign of the prophet Jonah." Then I left them. I got back into the boat and I crossed to the other side of the lake.

Later, the disciples discovered they had forgotten to bring any food, so there was only one loaf of bread with us on the boat. As we were crossing the lake, I warned them, "Beware of the yeast of the Pharisees and Sadducees and of Herod." They decided I was saying this because they hadn't brought any bread.

I knew what they were thinking, so I said, "You have so little faith! Why are you so worried about having no food? Won't you ever learn or understand? Are your hearts too hard to take it in?

> *You have eyes—can't you see? You have ears—can't you hear?*
>
> Jer. 5:21

Don't you remember anything at all?

"What about the five thousand men I fed with five loaves of bread? How many baskets of leftovers did you pick up?"

"Twelve," they said.

"And when I fed the four thousand with seven loaves, how many large baskets of leftovers did you pick up afterward?"

"Seven," they said.

I asked them, "Don't you understand even yet? How could you even think I was talking about food? So again I say, 'Beware of the yeast of the Pharisees and Sadducees.'"

Then at last they understood that I wasn't speaking about yeast or bread but about the false teaching of the Pharisees and Sadducees.

Mt. 16:1-12; Mk. 8:11-21

I Restored a Blind Man's Sight

Bethsaida

When we arrived at Bethsaida, some people brought a blind man to me, and they begged me to touch and heal the man. I took the blind man by the hand and led him out of the village. Then, spitting on the man's eyes, I laid my hands on him and asked, "Can you see anything now?"

The man looked around, "Yes," he said, "I see people, but I can't see them very clearly. They look like trees walking around."

Then I placed my hands over the man's eyes again. As the man stared intently, his eyesight was completely restored, and he could see everything clearly. I sent him home, saying, "Don't go back to the village on your way home."

Mk. 8:22-26

Simon Peter's Revelation and Rebuke

Caesarea Philippi, in the north country

My disciples and I left Galilee and went up to the villages of Caesarea Philippi.

One day as we were walking along, I asked them, "Who do people say the Son of Man is?"

"Well," they replied, "some say John the Baptist, some say Elijah, and others say you are Jeremiah or one of the other ancient prophets risen from the dead."

Then I asked them, "Who do you say that I am?"

Simon Peter answered, "You are the Messiah, the Son of the living God."

I replied, "You are blessed, Simon son of John, because my Father in heaven has revealed this to you. You did not learn this from any human being. Now I say to you that you are Peter, and upon this rock I will build my church, and all the powers of hell will not conquer it. And I will give you the keys of the Kingdom of Heaven. Whatever you lock on earth will be locked in heaven, and whatever you open on earth will be opened in heaven." Then I sternly warned them not to tell anyone that I was the Messiah.

From then on I began to tell my disciples plainly that I had to go to Jerusalem, and I told them what would happen to me there. "For I, the Son of Man, will suffer many terrible things," I said. "I will be rejected by the leaders, the leading priests, and the teachers of religious law. I will be killed, but three days later I will be raised from the dead."

But as I talked about this openly with my disciples, Peter took me aside and corrected me. "Heaven forbid, Lord," he said. "This will never happen to you!"

I turned and looked at my disciples and said to Peter very sternly, "Get away from me, Satan! You are a dangerous trap to me. You are seeing things merely from a human point of view, not from God's."

Then I called my disciples and the crowds to come over and listen. "If any of you wants to be my follower," I said, "you must put aside your selfish ambition, shoulder your cross daily, and follow me. If you try to keep your life for yourself, you will lose it. But if you give up your life for my sake and the sake of the Good News, you will find true life. And how do you benefit if you gain the whole world but lose or forfeit your own soul in the process? Is anything worth more than your soul?

"If a person is ashamed of me and my message in these adulterous and sinful days, I will be ashamed of that person when I return. For I, the Son of Man, will come in my glory and the glory of my Father with his holy angels and will judge all people according to their deeds."

And I went on to say, "I assure you that some of you standing here right now will not die before you see the Kingdom of God arrive in great power!"

Mt. 16:13-28; Mk. 8:27-9:1; Lu. 9:18-27

The Transfiguration

Six days later I took Peter and the two brothers, James and John, and led them up a high mountain to pray. No one else was there. As I was praying, the men watched. My appearance changed so that my face shone like the sun, and my clothing became dazzling white, far whiter than any earthly process could ever make it. Suddenly Moses and Elijah appeared and began talking with me. We were glorious to see. And we were speaking of how I was about to fulfill God's plan by dying in Jerusalem.

As Moses and Elijah were starting to leave, Peter blurted out, "Lord, this is wonderful! If you want me to, I'll make three shrines, * one for you, one for Moses, and one for Elijah." He really didn't know what he was saying, for they were all terribly afraid.

But even as he said it, a bright cloud came over them, and a voice from the cloud said, "This is my beloved Son, my chosen one, and I am fully pleased with him. Listen to him." The disciples were terrified and fell face down on the ground as it covered them.

When the voice died away, I came over and touched them. "Get up," I said, "don't be afraid." And when they looked around, Moses and Elijah were gone. They saw only me with them.

As we descended the mountainside, I commanded them, "Don't tell anyone what you have seen until I, the Son of Man, have risen from the dead." So they didn't tell anyone what they had seen until long after this happened. They kept it to themselves, but they often asked each other what I meant by "rising from the dead."

Now they began asking me, "Why do the teachers of religious law insist that Elijah must return before the Messiah comes?" I responded, "Elijah is indeed coming first to set everything in order. Why then is it written in the Scriptures that the Son of Man must suffer and be treated with utter contempt? But I tell you, Elijah has already come, but he wasn't recognized, and he was badly mistreated, just as the Scriptures predicted. And soon the Son of Man will also suffer at their hands." Then the disciples realized I had been speaking of John the Baptist.

Mt. 17:1-13; Mk. 9:2-13; Lu. 9:28-36

My Disciples Could Not Heal

The next day, when we arrived at the foot of the mountain, we found a great crowd surrounding the other disciples, as some teachers of religious law were arguing with them. The crowd watched me in awe as I came toward them, and they ran to greet me. "What is all this arguing about?" I asked.

One of the men in the crowd spoke up and said, "Teacher, look. I brought my boy, who is my only son, for you to heal him. He has seizures and suffers terribly. He can't speak because he is possessed by an evil spirit that won't let him talk. And whenever it seizes him, it throws him violently to the ground in convulsions and makes him foam at the mouth and grind his teeth and become rigid. This evil spirit is always hitting and injuring him, making him scream. It hardly leaves him alone. So I brought him to your disciples. I begged your disciples to cast the evil spirit out, but they couldn't heal him."

"You stubborn, faithless people!" I said to them. "How long must I be with you until you believe? How long must I put up with you? Bring the boy to me." So they brought the boy. But when the evil spirit saw me, it knocked the child to the ground and threw him into a violent convulsion, writhing and foaming at the mouth.

"How long has this been happening?" I asked the boy's father. He replied, "Since he was very small. The evil spirit often makes him fall into the fire or into the water, trying to kill him. Have mercy on us and help us. Do something if you can."

"What do you mean, 'If I can'?" I asked. "Anything is possible if a person believes." The father instantly replied, "I do believe, but help me not to doubt."

When I saw that the crowd of onlookers was growing, I rebuked the evil spirit. "Spirit of deafness and muteness," I said, "I command you to come out of this child and never enter him again!" Then the spirit screamed and threw the boy into another violent convulsion and left him. The boy lay there motionless, and he appeared to be dead. A murmur ran through the crowd. "He's dead." But I took him by the hand and helped him to his feet, and he stood up. Then

I gave him back to his father. From that moment the boy was well. Awe gripped the people as they saw this display of God's power.

Afterward, when I was alone in the house with my disciples, they asked me, "Why couldn't we cast out that evil spirit?"

"This kind can only be cast out by prayer," I replied. "You didn't have enough faith. I assure you," I told them, "even if you had faith as small as a mustard seed you could say to this mountain, 'Move from here to there,' and it would move. Nothing would be impossible."

Mt. 17:14-21; Mk. 9:14-29; Lu. 9:37-43a

I Predicted My Death

Galilee, on My Way to Capernaum

Leaving that region, we traveled through Galilee.

Everyone was marveling over all the wonderful things I was doing. I tried to avoid all publicity in order to spend more time with my disciples and teach them.

One day I told them, "Listen to me and remember what I say. The Son of Man is going to be betrayed. He will be killed, but three days later he will rise from the dead." And the disciples' hearts were filled with grief, but they didn't know what I meant. Its significance was hidden from them, so they could not understand it, and they were afraid to ask me about it.

On our arrival in Capernaum, the tax collectors for the Temple tax came to Peter and asked him, "Doesn't your teacher pay the Temple tax?"

"Of course he does," Peter replied. Then he came into the house to talk to me about it.

But before he got a chance to speak, I asked him, "What do you think, Peter? Do kings tax their own people or the foreigners they have conquered?"

"They tax foreigners," Peter replied.

"Well then," I said, "the citizens are free! However, we don't want to offend them, so go down to the lake and throw in a line. Open the mouth of the first fish you catch, and you will find a coin. Take the coin and pay the tax for both of us."

Mt. 17:22-27; Mk. 9:30-32; Lu. 9:43b-45

I Taught about the Kingdom

Summer, AD 29   Capernaum

After we arrived at Capernaum, my disciples and I settled in the house where we would be staying. I asked them, "What were you discussing out on the road?" But they didn't answer, because they had been arguing about which of them was the greatest. I sat down and called the twelve disciples over to me. Then the disciples asked, "Which of us is greatest in the Kingdom of Heaven?" I said, "Anyone who wants to be the first must take last place and be the servant of everyone else."

I called a small child over to me and put the child among them. "I assure you," I said, "unless you turn from your sins and become as little children, you will never get into the Kingdom of Heaven. Therefore, anyone who becomes as humble as this little child is the greatest in the Kingdom." Then, taking the child in my arms, I said to them, "Anyone who welcomes a little child like this on my behalf welcomes me, and anyone who welcomes me welcomes my Father who sent me. Whoever is least among you is the greatest. Beware that you don't despise a single one of these little ones. For I tell you that in heaven their angels are always in the presence of my heavenly Father.

"If a shepherd has one hundred sheep, and one wanders away and is lost, what will he do? Won't he leave the ninety-nine others and go out into the hills to search for the lost one? And if he finds it, he will surely rejoice over it more than over the ninety-nine that didn't wander away! In the same way, it is not my heavenly Father's will that even one of these little ones should perish."

John said to me, "Teacher, we saw a man using your name to cast out demons. We tried to stop him because he wasn't one of our group."

"Don't stop him!" I said. "No one who performs miracles in my name will soon be able to speak evil of me. Anyone who is not against us is for us. If anyone gives you even a cup of water because you belong to the Messiah, I assure you, that person will be rewarded.

"But if anyone causes one of these little ones who trusts in me to lose faith, it would be better for that person to be thrown into the sea with a large millstone tied around the neck.

"How terrible it will be for anyone who causes others to sin. Temptation to do wrong is inevitable, but how terrible it will be for the person who does the tempting. So if your hand or foot causes you to sin, cut it off and throw it away. It is better to enter heaven crippled or lame than to be thrown into the unquenchable fires of hell with both of your hands and feet. And if your eye causes you to sin, gouge it out and throw it away. It is better to enter the Kingdom of God half blind than to have two eyes and be thrown into hell,

where the worm never dies and the fire never goes out.

Isa. 66:24

For everyone will be purified with fire.

146

"Salt is good for seasoning. But if it loses its flavor, how do you make it salty again? You must have the qualities of salt among yourselves and live in peace with each other.

"If another believer sins against you, go privately and point out the fault. If the other person listens and confesses it, you have won that person back. But if you are unsuccessful, take one or two others with you and go back again, so that everything you say may be confirmed by two or three witnesses. If that person still refuses to listen, take your case to the church. If the church decides you are right, but the other won't accept it, treat that person as a pagan or a corrupt tax collector. I tell you this: Whatever you prohibit on earth is prohibited in heaven, and whatever you allow on earth is allowed in heaven.

"I also tell you this: If two of you agree down here on earth concerning anything you ask, my Father in heaven will do it for you. For where two or three gather together because they are mine, I am there among them."

Then Peter came to me and asked, "Lord, how often should I forgive someone who sins against me? Seven times?"

"No!" I replied, "seventy times seven!

"For this reason, the Kingdom of Heaven can be compared to a king who decided to bring his accounts up to date with servants who had borrowed money from him. In the process, one of his debtors was brought in who owed him millions of dollars. He couldn't pay, so the king ordered that he, his wife, his children, and everything he had be sold to pay the debt. But the man fell down before the king and begged him, 'Oh, sir, be patient with me, and I will pay it all.' Then the king was filled with pity for him, and he released him and forgave his debt.

"But when the man left the king, he went to a fellow servant who owed him a few thousand dollars. He grabbed him by the throat and demanded instant payment. His fellow servant fell down before him and begged for a little more time. 'Be patient and I will pay it,' he pleaded. But his creditor wouldn't wait. He had the man arrested and jailed until the debt could be paid in full.

"When some of the other servants saw this, they were very upset. They went to the king and told him what had happened. Then the king called in the man he had forgiven and said, 'You evil servant! I forgave you that tremendous debt because you pleaded with me. Shouldn't you have mercy on your fellow servant, just as I had mercy on you?' Then the angry king sent the man to prison until he had paid every penny.

"That's what my heavenly Father will do to you if you refuse to forgive your brothers and sisters in your heart."

Mt. 18:1-35; Mk. 9:33-50; Lu. 9:46-50

147

MY
THIRD VISIT
TO JERUSALEM
FALL, AD 29

THE
FESTIVAL OF SHELTERS
(IN JERUSALEM)
OCTOBER, AD 29

I Was Urged to Go to Jerusalem

October, AD 29

Soon it was time for the Festival of Shelters, and my brothers urged me to go to Judea for the celebration.

"Go where your followers can see your miracles!" they scoffed. "You can't become a public figure if you hide like this! If you can do such wonderful things, prove it to the world!" For even my brothers didn't believe in me.

I replied, "Now is not the right time for me to go. But you can go anytime, and it will make no difference. The world can't hate you, but it does hate me because I accuse it of sin and evil. You go on. I am not yet ready to go to this festival, because my time has not yet come. So I remained in Galilee.

But after my brothers had left for the festival, I also went, though secretly, staying out of public view. I left Capernaum and went southward to the region of Judea.

Mk. 10:1a; Jo. 7:2-10

We Stopped at Mary and Martha's Home

Bethany

As the disciples and I continued on our way to Jerusalem, we came to a village where a woman named Martha welcomed us into her home.

Her sister, Mary, sat at my feet listening to what I taught. But Martha was worrying over the big dinner she was preparing. She came to me and said, "Lord, doesn't it seem unfair to you that my sister just sits here while I do all the work? Tell her to come and help me."

But I said to her, "My dear Martha, you are so upset over all these details! There is really only one thing worth being concerned about. Mary has discovered it—and I won't take it away from her."

Lu. 10.38-42

The Festival in Jerusalem

The Jewish leaders tried to find me at the festival and kept asking if anyone had seen me. There was a lot of discussion about me among the crowds. Some said, "He's a wonderful man," while others said, "He's nothing but a fraud, deceiving the people." But no one had the courage to speak favorably about me in public, for they were afraid of getting in trouble with the Jewish leaders.

Then midway through the festival, I went up to the Temple and began to teach. The Jewish leaders were surprised when they heard me. "How does he know so much when he hasn't studied everything we've studied?" they asked.

So I told them, "I'm not teaching my own ideas, but those of God who sent me. Anyone who wants to do the will of God will know whether my teaching is from God or is merely my own. Those who present their own ideas are looking for praise for themselves, but those who seek to honor the one who sent them are good and genuine. None of you obeys the law of Moses! In fact, you are trying to kill me."

The crowd replied, "You're demon possessed! Who's trying to kill you?"

I replied, "I worked on the Sabbath by healing a man, and you were offended. But you work on the Sabbath, too, when you obey Moses' law of circumcision. (Actually, this tradition of circumcision is older than the law of Moses; it goes back to Abraham.) For if the correct time for circumcising your son falls on the Sabbath, you go ahead and do it, so as not to break the law of Moses. So why should I be condemned for making a man completely well on the Sabbath? Think this through and you will see that I am right."

Some of the people who lived there in Jerusalem said among themselves, "Isn't this the man they are trying to kill? But here he is, speaking in public, and they say nothing to him. Can it be that our leaders know that he really is the Messiah? But how could he be? For we know where this man comes from. When the Messiah comes, he will simply appear; no one will know where he comes from."

While I was teaching in the Temple, I called out, "Yes, you know me, and you know where I come from. But I represent one you do not know, and he is true. I know him because I have come from him, and he sent me to you." Then the leaders tried to arrest me; but no one laid a hand on me, because my time had not yet come.

Many among the crowds at the Temple believed in me. "After all," they said, "would you expect the Messiah to do more miraculous signs than this man has done?"

When the Pharisees heard that the crowds were murmuring such things, they and the leading priests sent Temple guards to arrest me. But I told them, "I will be here a little longer. Then I will return to the one who sent me. You will search for me but not find me. And you won't be able to come where I am."

The Jewish leaders were puzzled by this statement. "Where is he planning to go?" they asked. "Maybe he is thinking of leaving the country and going to the Jews in other lands, or maybe even to the

Gentiles! What does he mean when he says, 'You will search for me but not find me' and 'You won't be able to come where I am'?"

Jo. 7:11-36

The Final Day of the Festival

On the last day, the climax of the festival, I stood and shouted to the crowds, "If you are thirsty, come to me! If you believe in me, come and drink! For the Scriptures declare that rivers of living water will flow out from within." (When I said, "living water," I was speaking of the Spirit, who would be given to everyone believing in me. But the Spirit had not yet been given, because I had not yet entered into my glory.)

When the crowds heard me say this, some of them declared, "This man surely is the Prophet." Others said, "He is the Messiah." Still others said, "But he can't be! Will the Messiah come from Galilee? For the Scriptures clearly state that the Messiah will be born of the royal line, in Bethlehem, the village where King David was born." So the crowd was divided in their opinion about me. And some wanted me arrested, but no one touched me.

The Temple guards who had been sent to arrest me returned to the leading priests and Pharisees. "Why didn't you bring him in?" they demanded.

"We have never heard anyone talk like this!" the guards responded.

"Have you been led astray, too?" the Pharisees mocked. "Is there a single one of us rulers or Pharisees who believes in him? These ignorant crowds do, but what do they know about it? A curse on them anyway!"

Nicodemus, the leader who had met with me earlier, then spoke up. "Is it legal to convict a man before he is given a hearing?" he asked.

They replied, "Are you from Galilee, too? Search the Scriptures and see for yourself—no prophet ever comes from Galilee!" Then the meeting broke up and everybody went home.

Jo. 7:37-53

THE
RELIGIOUS LEADERS
IN JERUSALEM
WERE
ANTAGONIZED
BY ME

I Encounter an Adulterous Woman

The Temple

I returned to the Mount of Olives, but early the next morning I was back again at the Temple. A crowd soon gathered, and I sat down and taught them. As I was speaking, the teachers of religious law and Pharisees had brought a woman they had caught in the act of adultery. They put her in front of the crowd.

"Teacher," they said to me, "this woman was caught in the very act of adultery. The law of Moses says to stone her. What do you say?"

They were trying to trap me into saying something they could use against me, but I stooped down and wrote in the dust with my finger. They kept demanding an answer, so I stood up again and said, "All right, stone her. But let those who have never sinned throw the first stones!" Then I stooped down again and wrote in the dust.

When the accusers heard this, they slipped away one by one, beginning with the oldest, until only I was left in the middle of the crowd with the woman. Then I stood up again and said to her, "Where are your accusers? Didn't even one of them condemn you?"

"No, Lord," she said.

And I said, "Neither do I. Go and sin no more."

Jo. 8:1-11

I Was Sent by My Father

I said to the people, "I am the light of the world. If you follow me, you won't be stumbling through darkness, because you will have the light that leads to life."

The Pharisees replied, "You are making false claims about yourself."

I told them, "These claims are valid even though I make them about myself. For I know where I came from and where I am going, but you don't know this about me. You judge me with all your human limitations, but I am not judging anyone. And if I did, my judgment would be correct in every respect because I am not alone— I have with me the Father who sent me. Your own law says that if two people agree about something, their witness is accepted as fact. I am one witness, and my Father who sent me is the other."

"Where is your father?" they asked.

I answered, "Since you do not know who I am, you do not now who my Father is. If you knew me, then you would know my Father, too." I made these statements while I was teaching in the section of

159

the Temple known as the Treasury. But I was not arrested, because my time had not yet come.

Later I said to them again, "I am going away. You will search for me and die in your sin. You cannot come where I am going."

The Jewish leaders asked, "Is he planning to commit suicide? What does he mean, 'You cannot come where I am going'?"

Then I said to them, "You are from below; I am from above. You are of this world; I am not. That is why I said that you will die in your sins; for unless you believe that I am who I say I am, you will die in your sins."

"Tell us who you are," they demanded.

I replied, "I am the one I have always claimed to be. I have much to say about you and much to condemn, but I won't. For I say only what I have heard from the one who sent me, and he is true."

But they still didn't understand that I was talking to them about the Father.

So I said, "When you have lifted up the Son of Man on the cross, then you will realize that I am he and that I do nothing on my own, but I speak what the Father taught me. And the one who sent me is with me—he has not deserted me. For I always do those things that are pleasing to him." Then many who heard me say these things believed in me.

I said to the people who believed in me, "You are truly my disciples if you keep obeying my teachings.* And you will know the truth, and the truth will set you free."

"But we are descendants of Abraham," they said. "We have never been slaves to anyone on earth. What do you mean, 'set free'?"

I replied, "I assure you that everyone who sins is a slave of sin. A slave is not a permanent member of the family, but a son is part of the family forever. So if the Son sets you free, you will indeed be free. Yes, I realize that you are descendants of Abraham. And yet some of you are trying to kill me because my message does not find a place in your hearts. I am telling you what I saw when I was with my Father. But you are following the advice of your father."

"Our father is Abraham," they declared.

"No," I said, "for if you were children of Abraham, you would follow his good example. I told you the truth which I heard from God, but you are trying to kill me. Abraham wouldn't do a thing like that. No, you are obeying your real father when you act that way."

They replied, "We were not born out of wedlock! Our true Father is God himself."

I told them, "If God were your Father, you would love me, because I have come to you from God. I am not here on my own, but he sent me. Why can't you understand what I am saying? It is because you are unable to do so! For you are the children of your father the devil, and you love to do the evil things he does. He was a murderer from the beginning and has always hated the truth. There is no truth in him. When he lies, it is consistent with his character; for he is a liar and the father of lies. So when I tell the truth, you just naturally don't believe me! Which of you can truthfully accuse me of sin? And since I am telling you the truth, why don't you believe me? Anyone whose Father is God listens gladly to the words of God. Since you don't, it proves you aren't God's children."

The people retorted, "You Samaritan devil! Didn't we say all along that you were possessed by a demon?"

"No," I said, "I have no demon in me. For I honor my Father—and you dishonor me. And though I have no wish to glorify myself, God wants to glorify me. Let him be the judge. I assure you, anyone who obeys my teaching will never die!"

The people said, "Now we know you are possessed by a demon. Even Abraham and the prophets died, but you say that those who obey your teachings will never die! Are you greater than our father Abraham, who died? Are you greater than the prophets, who died? Who do you think you are?"

I answered, "If I am merely boasting about myself, it doesn't count. But it is my Father who says these glorious things about me. You say, 'He is our God,' but you do not even know him. I know him. If I said otherwise, I would be as great a liar as you! But it is true—I know him and obey him. Your ancestor Abraham rejoiced as he looked forward to my coming. He saw it and was glad."

The people said, "You aren't even fifty years old. How can you say you have seen Abraham?"

I answered, "The truth is, I existed before Abraham was even born!" At that point they picked up stones to kill me. But I hid myself from them and left the Temple.

Jo. 8:12-59

I Healed a Blind Beggar

As I was walking along, I saw a man who had been blind from birth. "Teacher," my disciples asked me, "why was this man born blind? Was it a result of his own sins or those of his parents?"

"It was not because of his sins or his parents' sins." I answered. "He was born blind so the power of God could be seen in him. All of us must quickly carry out the tasks assigned us by the one who sent me,* because there is little time left before the night falls and all work comes to an end. But while I am still here in the world, I am the light of the world."

Then I spit on the ground, made mud with the saliva, and smoothed the mud over the blind man's eyes. I told him, "Go wash in the pool of Siloam." (Siloam means sent.) So the man went and washed, and came back seeing!

His neighbors and others who knew him as a blind beggar asked each other, "Is this the same man—that beggar?" Some said he was, and others said, "No, but he surely looks like him!" And the beggar kept saying, "I am the same man!"

They asked, "Who healed you? What happened?"

He told them, "The man they call Jesus made mud and smoothed it over my eyes and told me, 'Go to the pool of Siloam and wash off the mud.' I went and washed, and now I can see!"

"Where is he now?" they asked.

"I don't know," he replied.

Then they took the man to the Pharisees. Now as it happened, I had healed the man on a Sabbath. The Pharisees asked the man all about it. So he told them, "He smoothed the mud over my eyes, and when it was washed away, I could see."

Some of the Pharisees said, "This man Jesus is not from God, for he is working on the Sabbath." Others said, "But how could an ordinary sinner do such miraculous signs?" So there was a deep division of opinion among them.

Then the Pharisees once again questioned the man who had been blind and demanded, "This man who opened your eyes—who do you say he is?" The man replied, "I think he must be a prophet."

The Jewish leaders wouldn't believe he had been blind, so they called in his parents. They asked them, "Is this your son? Was he born blind? If so, how can he see?"

His parents replied, "We know our son and that he was born blind, but we don't know how he can see or who healed him. He is old enough to speak for himself. Ask him."

They said this because they were afraid of the Jewish leaders, who had announced that anyone saying I was the Messiah would be expelled from the synagogue. That's why they said, "He is old enough to speak for himself. Ask him."

So for the second time they called in the man who had been blind and told him, "Give glory to God by telling the truth, because we know Jesus is a sinner."

"I don't know whether he is a sinner," the man replied. "But I know this; I was blind, and now I can see!"

"But what did he do?" they asked. How did he heal you?"

"Look!" the man exclaimed. "I told you once. Didn't you listen? Why do you want to hear it again? Do you want to become his disciples, too?"

Then they cursed him and said, "You are his disciple, but we are disciples of Moses. We know God spoke to Moses; but as for this man, we don't know anything about him"

"Why, that's very strange!" The man replied. "He healed my eyes, and yet you don't know anything about him! Well, God doesn't listen to sinners, but he is ready to hear those who worship him and do his will. Never since the world began has anyone been able to open the eyes of someone born blind. If this man were not from God, he couldn't do it."

"You were born in sin!" they answered. "Are you trying to teach us?" And they threw him out of the synagogue.

When I heard what had happened, I found the man and said, "Do you believe in the Son of Man?"

The man answered, "Who is he, sir, because I would like to."

"You have seen him," I said, "and he is speaking to you!"

"Yes, Lord," the man said, "I believe!" And he worshiped me.

Then I told him, "I have come to judge the world. I have come to give sight to the blind and to show those who think they see that they are blind."

The Pharisees who were standing there heard me and asked, "Are you saying we are blind?"

"If you were blind, you wouldn't be guilty," I replied. "But you remain guilty because you claim you can see."

Jo. 9:1-41

I Am the Good Shepherd

"I assure you, anyone who sneaks over the wall of a sheepfold, rather than going through the gate, must surely be a thief and a robber! For a shepherd enters through the gate. The gatekeeper opens the gate for him, and the sheep hear his voice and come to him. He calls his own sheep by name and leads them out. After he has gathered his own flock, he walks ahead of them, and they follow him because they recognize his voice. They won't follow a stranger; they will run from him because they don't recognize his voice."

Those who heard me use this illustration didn't understand what I meant, so I explained it to them. "I assure you, I am the gate for the sheep." I said. "All others who came before me were thieves and robbers. But the true sheep did not listen to them. Yes, I am the gate. Those who come in through me will be saved. Wherever they go, they will find green pastures. The thief's purpose is to steal and kill and destroy. My purpose is to give life in all its fullness.

"I am the good shepherd. The good shepherd lays down his life for the sheep. A hired hand will run when he sees a wolf coming. He will leave the sheep because they aren't his and he isn't their shepherd. And so the wolf attacks and scatters the flock. The hired hand runs away because he is merely hired and has no real concern for the sheep.

"I am the good shepherd; I know my own sheep, and they know me, just as my Father knows me and I know the Father. And I lay down my life for the sheep. I have other sheep, too, that are not in this sheepfold. I must bring them also, and they will listen to my voice, and there will be one flock with one shepherd.

"The Father loves me because I lay down my life that I may have it back again. No one can take my life from me. I lay down my life voluntarily. For I have the right to lay it down when I want to and also the power to take it again. For my Father has given me this command."

When I said these things, the people were again divided in their opinion about me. Some of them said, "He has a demon, or he's crazy. Why listen to a man like that?" Others said, "This doesn't sound like a man possessed by a demon! Can a demon open the eyes of the blind?"

Jo. 10:1-21

The Jewish Leaders Tried to Kill Me

December, AD 29

It was now winter, and I was in Jerusalem at the time of Hanukkah.*

I was at the Temple, walking through the section known as Solomon's Colonnade. The Jewish leaders surrounded me and asked, "How long are you going to keep us in suspense? If you are the Messiah, tell us plainly."

I replied, "I have already told you, and you don't believe me. The proof is what I do in the name of my Father. But you don't believe me because you are not part of my flock. My sheep recognize my voice; I know them, and they follow me. I give them eternal life, and they will never perish. No one will snatch them away from me, for my Father has given them to me, and he is more powerful than anyone else. So no one can take them from me. The Father and I are one."

Once again the Jewish leaders picked up stones to kill me. I said, "At my Father's direction I have done many things to help the people. For which one of these good deeds are you killing me?"

They replied, "Not for any good work, but for blasphemy, because you, a mere man, have made yourself God."

I replied, "It is written in your own law that God said to certain leaders of the people,

I say, you are gods!

Ps. 82:6

And you know that the Scriptures cannot be altered. So if those people, who received God's message, were called 'gods,' why do you call it blasphemy when the Holy One who was sent into the world by the Father says, 'I am the Son of God'? Don't believe me unless I carry out my Father's work. But if I do his work, believe in what I have done, even if you don't believe me. Then you will realize that the Father is in me, and I am in the Father."

Once again they tried to arrest me, but I got away and left them. I went beyond the Jordan River to stay near the place where John was first baptizing. And many followed me. "John didn't do miracles," they remarked to one another, "but all his predictions about this man have come true." And many believed in me there.

Jo. 10:22-42

PART V

I
BEGAN THE
LAST YEAR
OF MY
MINISTRY

AD 30

I
MINISTERED
THROUGHOUT
THE LAND
ONE LAST TIME

I Taught My Disciples about Prayer

Early AD 30   Perea

Once when I had been out praying, one of my disciples came to me as I finished and said, "Lord, teach us to pray, just as John taught his disciples."

I said, "This is how you should pray:

"Father, may your name be honored. May your Kingdom come soon. Give us our food day by day. And forgive us our sins—just as we forgive those who have sinned against us. And don't let us yield to temptation."

Then teaching them more about prayer, I used this illustration: "Suppose you went to a friend's house at midnight, wanting to borrow three loaves of bread. You would say to him, 'A friend of mine has just arrived for a visit, and I have nothing for him to eat.' He would call out from his bedroom, 'Don't bother me. The door is locked for the night, and we are all in bed. I can't help you this time.' But I tell you this—though he won't do it as a friend, if you keep knocking long enough, he will get up and give you what you want so his reputation won't be damaged.

"And so I tell you, keep on asking, and you will be given what you ask for. Keep on looking, and you will find. Keep on knocking, and the door will be opened. For everyone who asks, receives. Everyone who seeks, finds. And the door is opened to everyone who knocks.

"You fathers—if your children ask for a fish, do you give them a snake instead? Or if they ask for an egg, do you give them a scorpion? Of course not! If you sinful people know how to give good gifts to your children, how much more will your heavenly Father give the Holy Spirit to those who ask him."

Lu. 11:1-13

MY
FRIEND
LAZARUS

I Raised My Friend Lazarus from Death

Bethany

A man named Lazarus was sick. He lived in Bethany with his sisters, Mary and Martha. This is the Mary who poured the expensive perfume on my feet and wiped them with her hair. Her brother, Lazarus, was sick, so the two sisters sent a message to me telling me, "Lord, the one you love is very sick."

But when I heard about it I said, "Lazarus' sickness will not end in death. No, it is for the glory of God. I, the Son of God, will receive glory from this."

Although I loved Martha, Mary, and Lazarus, I stayed where I was for the next two days and did not go to them. Finally after two days, I said to my disciples, "Let's go to Judea again."

But my disciples objected. "Teacher," they said, "only a few days ago the Jewish leaders in Judea were trying to kill you. Are you going there again?"

I replied, "There are twelve hours of daylight every day. As long as it is light, people can walk safely. They can see because they have the light of this world. Only at night is there danger of stumbling because there is no light." Then I said, "Our friend Lazarus has fallen asleep, but now I will go and wake him up."

The disciples said, "Lord, if he is sleeping, that means he is getting better." They thought I meant Lazarus was having a good night's rest, but I meant Lazarus had died.

Then I told them plainly, "Lazarus is dead. And for your sake, I am glad I wasn't there, because this will give you another opportunity to believe in me. Come, let's go see him."

Thomas, nicknamed the Twin, said to his fellow disciples, "Let's go, too—and die with Jesus."

When I arrived at Bethany, I was told that Lazarus had already been in his grave four days. Bethany was only a few miles down the road from Jerusalem, and many people had come to pay their respects and console Martha and Mary on their loss. When Martha got word that I was coming, she came to meet me. But Mary stayed at home. Martha said to me, "Lord, if you had been here, my brother would not have died. But even now I know that God will give you whatever you ask."

I told her, "Your brother will rise again."

"Yes," Martha said, "when everyone else rises on resurrection day."

I told her, "I am the resurrection and the life. Those who believe in me, even though they die like everyone else, will live again. They

175

are given eternal life for believing in me and will never perish. Do you believe this Martha?"

"Yes, Lord," she told me. "I have always believed you are the Messiah, the Son of God, the one who has come into the world from God." Then she left me and returned to Mary. She called Mary aside from the mourners and told her, "The Teacher is here and wants to see you." So Mary immediately came to me.

Now I had stayed outside the village, at the place where Martha met me. When the people who were at the house trying to console Mary saw her leave so hastily, they assumed she was going to Lazarus' grave to weep. So they followed her there. When Mary arrived and saw me, she fell down at my feet and said, "Lord, if you had been here, my brother would not have died."

When I saw her weeping and saw the other people wailing with her, I was moved with indignation* and was deeply troubled. "Where have you put him?" I asked them.

They told me, "Lord, come and see." Then I wept. The people who were standing nearby said, "See how much he loved him." But some said, "This man healed a blind man. Why couldn't he keep Lazarus from dying?"

And again I was deeply troubled. Then we came to the grave. It was a cave with a stone rolled across its entrance.

"Roll the stone aside," I told them. But Martha, the dead man's sister, said, "Lord, by now the smell will be terrible because he has been dead for four days."

I responded, "Didn't I tell you that you will see God's glory if you believe?" So they rolled the stone aside. Then I looked up to heaven and said, "Father, thank you for hearing me. You always hear me, but I said it out loud for the sake of all these people standing here, so they will believe you sent me."

Then I shouted, "Lazarus, come out!" And Lazarus came out, bound in graveclothes, his face wrapped in a headcloth. I told them, "Unwrap him and let him go!"

Many of the people who were with Mary believed in me when they saw this happen. But some went to the Pharisees and told them what I had done. Then the leading priests and Pharisees called the high council together to discuss the situation. "What are we going to do?" they asked each other. "This man certainly performs many miraculous signs. If we leave him alone, the whole nation will follow him, and then the Roman army will come and destroy both our Temple and our nation."

And one of them, Caiaphas, who was high priest that year, said, "How can you be so stupid? Why should the whole nation be destroyed? Let this one man die for the people."

This prophecy that I should die for the entire nation came from Caiaphas in his position as high priest. He didn't think of it himself; he was inspired to say it. It was a prediction that my death would be not for Israel only, but for the gathering together of all the children of God scattered around the world.

So from that time on the Jewish leaders began to plot my death. As a result, I stopped my public ministry among the people and left Jerusalem. I went to a place near the wilderness, to the village of Ephraim, and stayed there with my disciples.

Jo. 11:1-54

I Was Once More Rejected in My Home Town

Nazareth

I left that part of the country and returned with my disciples to Nazareth, my home town.

The next Sabbath I began teaching in the synagogue, and many who heard me were astonished and said, "Where does he get his wisdom and the power to perform miracles? He's just a carpenter's son, and we know Mary, his mother, and his brothers—James, Joseph, Simon, and Judas. All his sisters live right here among us. What makes him so great?" They were deeply offended and refused to believe in me.

Then I told them, "A prophet is honored everywhere except in his own hometown and among his relatives and his own family." And because of their unbelief, I couldn't do any mighty miracles among them except to place my hands on a few sick people and heal them. And I was amazed at their unbelief.

Mt. 13:53b-58; Mk. 6:1-6a

I
RETURNED TO
CAPERNAUM

I Sent Out Seventy-Two Disciples

I now chose seventy-two other disciples and sent them on ahead in pairs to all the towns and villages I planned to visit. These were my instructions to them:

"The harvest is so great, but the workers are so few. Pray to the Lord who is in charge of the harvest, and ask him to send out more workers for his fields. Go now, and remember that I am sending you out as lambs among wolves. Don't take along any money, or a traveler's bag, or even an extra pair of sandals. And don't stop to greet anyone on the road.

"Whenever you enter a town, give your blessing. If those who live there are worthy, the blessing will stand; if they are not, the blessing will return to you. When you enter a town, don't move around from home to home. Stay in one place, eating and drinking what they provide for you. Don't hesitate to accept hospitality, because those who work deserve their pay.

"If a town welcomes you, eat whatever is set before you and heal the sick. As you heal them, say 'The Kingdom of God is near you now.' But if a town refuses to welcome you, go out into its streets and say, 'We wipe the dust of your town from our feet as a public announcement of your doom. And don't forget the Kingdom of God is near!' The truth is, even wicked Sodom will be better off than such a town on the judgment day.

I began to denounce the cities where I had done most of my miracles, because they hadn't turned from their sins and turned to God. "What horrors await you, Korazin and Bethsaida! For if the miracles I did in you had been done in wicked Tyre and Sidon, their people would have sat in deep repentance long ago, clothed in sackcloth and throwing ashes on their heads to show their remorse. I assure you, Tyre and Sidon will be better off on the judgment day than you.

"And you people of Capernaum, will you be exalted to heaven? No, you will be brought down to the place of the dead. For if the miracles I did for you had been done in Sodom, it would still be here today. I assure you, Sodom will be better off on the judgment day than you."

Then I said to the disciples, "Anyone who accepts your message is also accepting me. And anyone who rejects you is rejecting me. And anyone who rejects me is rejecting God who sent me."

When the seventy-two disciples returned, they joyfully reported to me, "Lord, even the demons obey us when we use your name!"

"Yes," I told them, "I saw Satan falling from heaven as a flash of lightning! And I have given you authority over all the power of the enemy, and you can walk among snakes and scorpions and crush them. Nothing will injure you. But don't rejoice just because evil spirits obey you; rejoice because your names are registered as citizens of heaven."

Then I was filled with the joy of the Holy Spirit and prayed this prayer:

"O Father, Lord of heaven and earth, thank you for hiding the truth from those who think themselves so wise and clever, and for revealing it to the childlike. Yes, Father, it pleased you to do it this way.

"My Father has given me authority over everything. No one really knows the Son except the Father, and no one really knows the Father except the Son and those to whom the Son chooses to reveal him."

Then I said, "Come to me, all of you who are weary and carry heavy burdens, and I will give you rest. Take my yoke upon you. Let me teach you, because I am humble and gentle, and you will find rest for your souls. For my yoke fits perfectly, and the burden I give you is light."

Then when we were alone, I turned to the disciples and said, "How privileged you are to see what you have seen. I tell you, many prophets and kings have longed to see and hear what you have seen and heard, but they could not."

Mt. 11:20-30; Lu. 10:1-24

The Religious Experts Tested Me

One day an expert in religious law stood up to test me by asking me this question: "Teacher, what must I do to receive eternal life?" I replied, "What does the law of Moses say? How do you read it?"

The man answered,

You must love the Lord your God with all your heart, all your soul, all your strength, and all your mind.

Deut. 6:5

And,

Love your neighbor as yourself.

Lev. 19:18

"Right," I told him. "Do this and you will live!"

The man wanted to justify his actions, so he asked me, "And who is my neighbor?"

I replied with an illustration:

"A Jewish man was traveling on a trip from Jerusalem to Jericho, and he was attacked by bandits. They stripped him of his clothes and money, beat him up, and left him half dead beside the road.

182

"By chance a Jewish priest came along; but when he saw the man lying there, he crossed to the other side of the road and passed him by. A Temple assistant* walked over and looked at him lying there, but he also passed by on the other side.

"Then a despised Samaritan came along, and when he saw the man, he felt deep pity. Kneeling beside him, the Samaritan soothed his wounds with medicine and bandaged them. Then he put the man on his own donkey and took him to an inn, where he took care of him. The next day he handed the innkeeper two pieces of silver and told him to take care of the man. 'If his bill runs higher than that,' he said, 'I'll pay the difference the next time I am here.'

"Now which of these three would you say was a neighbor to the man who was attacked by bandits?" I asked.

The man replied, "The one who showed him mercy."

Then I said, "Yes, now go and do the same."

Lu. 10:25-37

I
CONTINUED
TO MINISTER—
HEALING THE SICK
AND
TEACHING ABOUT
THE KINGDOM

I Again Healed on the Sabbath

On the Sabbath day I was in the home of a leader of the Pharisees. The people were watching me closely, because there was a man there whose arms and legs were swollen. I asked the Pharisees and experts in religious law, "Well, is it permitted in the law to heal people on the Sabbath Day, or not?"

When they refused to answer, I touched the sick man and healed him and sent him away. Then I turned to them and asked, "Which of you doesn't work on the Sabbath? If your son or your cow falls into a pit, don't you proceed at once to get him out?" Again they had no answer.

Lu. 14:1-6

I Continued Teaching with Many Parables

When I noticed that all who had come to the dinner were trying to sit near the head of the table, I gave them this advice:

"If you are invited to a wedding feast, don't always head for the best seat. What if someone more respected than you has also been invited? Then the host will say, 'Let this person sit here instead.' Then you will be embarrassed and will have to take whatever seat is left at the foot of the table!

"Do this instead—sit at the foot of the table. Then when your host sees you, he will come and say, 'Friend, we have a better place than this for you!' Then you will be honored in front of all the other guests. For the proud will be humbled, but the humble will be honored."

Then I turned to my host. "When you put on a luncheon or a dinner," I said, "don't invite your friends, brothers, relatives, and rich neighbors. For they will repay you by inviting you back. Instead, invite the poor, the crippled, the lame, and the blind. Then at the resurrection of the godly, God will reward you for inviting those who could not repay you."

Hearing this, a man sitting at the table with me exclaimed, "What a privilege it would be to have a share in the Kingdom of God!"

The story about excuses

I replied with this illustration: "A man prepared a great feast and sent out many invitations. When all was ready, he sent his servant around to notify the guests that it was time for them to come. But they all began making excuses. One said he had just bought a field and wanted to inspect it, so he asked to be excused. Another said he had just bought five pair of oxen and wanted to try them out. Another had just been married, so he said he couldn't come.

"The servant returned and told his master what they had said. His master was angry and said, 'Go quickly into the streets and alleys of the city and invite the poor, the crippled, the lame, and the blind.' After the servant had done this, he reported, 'There is still room for more.' So his master said, 'Go out into the country lanes and behind the hedges and urge anyone you find to come, so that the house will be full. For none of those I invited first will get even the smallest taste of what I had prepared for them.'"

The cost of discipleship

Great crowds were following me. I turned around and said to them, "If you want to be my follower you must love me more than your own father and mother, wife and children, brothers and sisters—yes, more than your own life. Otherwise, you cannot be my disciple. And you cannot be my disciple if you do not carry your own cross and follow me.

"But don't begin until you count the cost. For who would begin construction of a building without first getting estimates and then checking to see if there is enough money to pay the bills? Otherwise, you might complete only the foundation before running out of funds. And then how everyone would laugh at you! They would say, 'There's the person who started that building and ran out of money before it was finished!'

"Or what king would ever dream of going to war without first sitting down with his counselors and discussing whether his army of ten thousand is strong enough to defeat the twenty thousand soldiers who are marching against him? If he is not able, then while the enemy is still far away, he will send a delegation to discuss terms of peace. So no one can become my disciple without giving up everything for me."

Saltless salt

"Salt is good for seasoning. But if it loses its flavor, how do you make it salty again? Flavorless salt is good neither for the soil nor for fertilizer. It is thrown away. Anyone who is willing to hear should listen and understand!"

The sheperd's one lost sheep

Tax collectors and other notorious sinners often came to listen to me teach. This made the Pharisees and teachers of religious law complain that I was associating with such despicable people—even eating with them! So I used this illustration:

"If you had one hundred sheep, and one of them strayed away and was lost in the wilderness, wouldn't you leave the ninety-nine others to go and search for the lost one until you found it? And then you would joyfully carry it home on your shoulders. When you arrived, you would call together your friends and neighbors to rejoice with you because your lost sheep was found. In the same way, heaven will be happier over one lost sinner who returns to God than over ninety-nine others who are righteous and haven't strayed away!"

The lost coin

"Or suppose a woman has ten valuable silver coins and loses one. Won't she light a lamp and look in every corner of the house and sweep every nook and cranny until she finds it? And when she finds it, she will call in her friends and neighbors to rejoice with her because she has found her lost coin. In the same way, there is joy in the presence of God's angels when even one sinner repents."

The wayward son's forgiving father

To illustrate the point further, I told them this story: "A man had two sons. The younger son told his father, 'I want my share of your estate now, instead of waiting until you die.' So his father agreed to divide his wealth between his sons.

"A few days later this younger son packed all his belongings and took a trip to a distant land, and there he wasted all his money on wild living. About the time his money ran out, a great famine swept over the land, and he began to starve. He persuaded a local farmer to hire him to feed his pigs. The boy became so hungry that even the pods he was feeding the pigs looked good to him. But no one gave him anything.

"When he finally came to his senses, he said to himself, 'At home even the hired men have food enough to spare, and here I am, dying of hunger! I will go home to my father and say, 'Father, I have sinned against both heaven and you and I am no longer worthy of being called your son. Please take me on as a hired man.'

"So he returned home to his father. And while he was still a long distance away, his father saw him coming. Filled with love and compassion, he ran to his son, embraced him, and kissed him. His son said to him, 'Father, I have sinned against both heaven and you, and I am no longer worthy of being called your son.'

"But his father said to the servants, 'Quick! Bring the finest robe in the house and put it on him. Get a ring for his finger, and sandals for his feet. And kill the calf we have been fattening in the pen. We must celebrate with a feast, for this son of mine was dead and has now returned to life. He was lost, but now he is found.' So the party began.

"Meanwhile, the older son was in the fields working. When he returned home, he heard music and dancing in the house, and he asked one of the servants what was going on. 'Your brother is back,' he was told, 'and your father has killed the calf we were fattening and has prepared a great feast. We are celebrating because of his safe return.'

"The older brother was angry and wouldn't go in. His father came out and begged him, but he replied, 'All these years I've worked hard for you and never once refused to do a single thing you told me to do. And in all that time you never gave me even one young goat for a feast with my friends. Yet when this son of yours comes back after squandering your money on prostitutes, you celebrate by killing the finest calf we have.'

"His father said to him, 'Look, dear son, you and I are very close, and everything I have is yours. We had to celebrate this happy day. For your brother was dead and has come back to life! He was lost, but now he is found!'"

The shrewdness of this world

I told this story to my disciples: "A rich man hired a manager to handle his affairs, but soon a rumor went around that the manager was thoroughly dishonest. So his employer called him in and said, 'What's this I hear about your stealing from me? Get your report in order, because you are going to be dismissed.'

"The manager thought to himself, 'Now what? I'm through here, and I don't have the strength to go out and dig ditches, and I'm too proud to beg. I know just the thing! And then I'll have plenty of friends to take care of me when I leave!'

"So he invited each person who owed money to his employer to come and discuss the situation. He asked the first one, 'How much do you owe him?' The man replied, 'I owe him eight hundred gallons of olive oil.' So the manager told him, 'Tear up that bill and write another one for four hundred gallons.'

"'And how much do you owe my employer?' he asked the next man. 'A thousand bushels of wheat,' was the reply. 'Here,' the manager said, 'take your bill and replace it with one for only eight hundred bushels.'

"The rich man had to admire the dishonest rascal for being so shrewd. And it is true that the citizens of this world are more shrewd than the godly are.* I tell you, use your worldly resources to benefit others and make friends. In this way, your generosity stores up a reward for you in heaven."

Faithful over small things

"Unless you are faithful in small matters, you won't be faithful in large ones. If you cheat even a little, you won't be honest with greater responsibilities. And if you are untrustworthy about worldly wealth, who will trust you with the true riches of heaven? And if you are not faithful with other people's money, why should you be trusted with money of your own?

"No one can serve two masters. For you will hate one and love the other, or be devoted to one and despise the other. You cannot serve both God and money."

The Pharisees, who dearly loved their money, naturally scoffed at all this. Then I said to them, "You like to look good in public, but God knows your evil hearts. What this world honors is an abomination in the sight of God.

"Until John the Baptist began to preach, the law of Moses and the messages of the prophets were your guides. But now the Good News of the Kingdom of God is preached, and eager multitudes are forcing their way in. But that doesn't mean that the law has lost its force in even the smallest point. It is stronger and more permanent than heaven and earth.

A rich man lost; a poor man saved

"There was a certain rich man who was splendidly clothed and who lived each day in luxury. At his door lay a diseased beggar named Lazarus. As Lazarus lay there longing for scraps from the rich man's table, the dogs would come and lick his open sores. Finally, the beggar died and was carried by the angels to be with Abraham. The rich man also died and was buried, and his soul went to the place of the dead. There, in torment, he saw Lazarus in the far distance with Abraham.

"The rich man shouted, 'Father Abraham, have some pity! Send Lazarus over here to dip the tip of his finger in water and cool my tongue, because I am in anguish in these flames.'

"But Abraham said to him, 'Child, remember that during your lifetime you had everything you wanted, and Lazarus had nothing. So now he is here being comforted, and you are in anguish. And besides, there is a great chasm separating us. Anyone who wanted to cross over to you from here is stopped at its edge, and no one there can cross over to us.'

"Then the rich man said, 'Please, Father Abraham, send him to my father's home. For I have five brothers, and I want him to warn them about this place of torment so they won't have to come here when they die.'

"But Abraham said, 'Moses and the prophets have warned them. Your brothers can read their writings anytime they want to.'

"The rich man replied, 'No, Father Abraham! But if someone is sent to them from the dead, then they will turn from their sins.'

"But Abraham said, 'If they won't listen to Moses and the prophets, they won't listen even if someone rises from the dead.'"

The millstone

One day I said to my disciples, "There will always be temptations to sin, but how terrible it will be for the person who does the tempting. It would be better to be thrown into the sea with a millstone tied around the neck than to face the punishment in store for harming one of these little ones."

Forgiveness

"I am warning you! If another believer sins, rebuke him; then if he repents, forgive him. Even if he wrongs you seven times a day and each time turns again and asks forgiveness, forgive him."

A little faith is enough

One day the apostles said to me, "We need more faith; tell us how to get it."

"Even if you had faith as small as a mustard seed," I answered, "you could say to this mulberry tree, 'May God uproot you and throw you into the sea,' and it would obey you!"

The dutiful servant

"When a servant comes in from plowing or taking care of sheep, he doesn't just sit down and eat. He must first prepare his master's meal and serve him his supper before eating his own. And the servant is not even thanked, because he is merely doing what he is supposed to do. In the same way, when you obey me you should say, 'We are not worthy of praise. We are servants who have simply done our duty.'"

Lu.14:7-16:17, 19-17:10

I Prepared for My Last Journey to Jerusalem

Region beyond Judea

As the time drew near for my return to heaven, I resolutely set out for Jerusalem.

I sent messengers ahead to a Samaritan village to prepare for my arrival. But they were turned away. The people of the village refused to have anything to do with me because I had resolved to go to Jerusalem. When James and John heard about it, they said to me, "Lord, should we order down fire from heaven to burn them up?" But I turned and rebuked them.

So we went to another village. As we were walking along one of the teachers of religious law said to me, "Teacher, I will follow you no matter where you go!"

192

But I replied, "Foxes have dens to live in, and birds have nests; but I, the Son of Man, have no home of my own, not even a place to lay my head."

I said to another person, "Come, be my disciple." The man agreed, but he said, "Lord, first let me return home and bury my father."

I replied, "Follow me now. Let those who are spiritually dead care for their own dead. Your duty is to go and preach the coming of the Kingdom of God."

Another said, "Yes, Lord, I will follow you, but first let me say good-bye to my family."

But I told him, "Anyone who puts a hand to the plow and then looks back is not fit for the Kingdom of God."

Mt. 8:19-22; Lu. 9:51-62

I Continued to Heal the Sick

Early Spring, AD 30

As I continued on toward Jerusalem, I reached the border between Galilee and Samaria.

As I entered a village there, ten lepers stood at a distance, crying out, "Jesus, Master, have mercy on us!" I looked at them and said, "Go show yourselves to the priests." And as they went, their leprosy disappeared.

One of them, when he saw that he was healed, came back to me, shouting, "Praise God, I'm healed!" He fell face down on the ground at my feet, thanking me for what I had done. This man was a Samaritan.

I asked, "Didn't I heal ten men? Where are the other nine? Does only this foreigner return to give glory to God?" And I said to the man, "Stand up and go. Your faith has made you well."

Lu. 17:11-19

I Told of the Coming Kingdom

One day the Pharisees asked me, "When will the Kingdom of God come?" I replied, "The Kingdom of God isn't ushered in with visible signs. You won't be able to say, 'Here it is!' or 'It's over there!' For the Kingdom of God is among you." JESUS is THE Kingdom

Later I talked again about this with my disciples. "The time is coming when you will long to share in the days of the Son of Man, but you won't be able to," I said. "Reports will reach you that the Son of Man has returned and that he is in this place or that. Don't believe such reports or go out to look for him. For when the Son of

Man returns, you will know it beyond all doubt. It will be as evident as the lightning that flashes across the sky. But first the Son of Man must suffer terribly and be rejected by this generation.

"When the Son of Man returns, the world will be like the people were in Noah's day. In those days before the flood, the people enjoyed banquets and parties and weddings right up to the time Noah entered his boat and the flood came to destroy them all.

"And the world will be as it was in the days of Lot. People went about their daily business—eating and drinking, buying and selling, farming and building—until the morning Lot left Sodom. Then fire and burning sulfur rained down from heaven and destroyed them all.

"Yes, it will be 'business as usual' right up to the hour when the Son of Man returns. On that day a person outside the house must not go into the house to pack. A person in the field must not return to town. Remember what happened to Lot's wife! Whoever clings to this life will lose it, and whoever loses his life will save it. That night two people will be asleep in one bed; one will be taken away, and the other will be left. Two women will be grinding flour together at the mill; one will be taken, the other left." *one is saved*

"Lord, where will this happen?" the disciples asked. I replied, "Just as the gathering of vultures shows there is a carcass nearby, so these signs indicate that the end is near."

Lu. 17:20-37

I Spoke Again in Parables

The judge and the widow

One day I told my disciples a story to illustrate their need for constant prayer and to show them that they must never give up.

"There was a judge in a certain city," I said, "who was a godless man with great contempt for everyone. A widow of that city came to him repeatedly, appealing for justice against someone who had harmed her. The judge ignored her for awhile, but eventually she wore him out. 'I fear neither God nor man,' he said to himself, 'but this woman is driving me crazy. I'm going to see that she gets justice, because she is wearing me out with her constant requests!'"

Then I said, "Learn a lesson from this evil judge. Even he rendered a just decision in the end, so don't you think God will surely give justice to his chosen people who plead with him day and night? Will he keep putting them off? I tell you, he will grant justice to them quickly! But when I, the Son of Man, return, how many will I find who have faith?"

A good man lost; a bad man saved

Then I told this story to some who had great self-confidence and scorned everyone else: "Two men went to the Temple to pray. One was a Pharisee, and the other was a dishonest tax collector. The proud Pharisee stood by himself and prayed this prayer: 'I thank you, God, that I am not a sinner like everyone else, especially like that tax collector over there! For I never cheat, I don't sin, I don't commit adultery, I fast twice a week, and I give you a tenth of my income.'

"But the tax collector stood at a distance and dared not even lift his eyes to heaven as he prayed. Instead, he beat his chest in sorrow, saying, 'O God, be merciful to me, for I am a sinner.' I tell you, this sinner, not the Pharisee, returned home justified before God. For the proud will be humbled, but the humble will be honored."

Lu. 18:1-14

I Discussed Divorce

Judea

When I had finished telling these stories, I left Galilee and went southward to the region of Judea and into the area east of the Jordan River. As always, vast crowds followed me there; and as usual I taught them, and I healed their sick.

Some Pharisees came and tried to trap me with this question: "Should a man be allowed to divorce his wife for any reason?"

"What did Moses say about divorce?" I asked them.

"Well, he permitted it," they replied. "He said a man merely has to write his wife an official letter of divorce and send her away."

But I responded, "Haven't you read the Scriptures? God's plan was seen from the beginning of creation, for

> *God made them male and female.*

Gen. 1:27, 5:2

And Moses said,

> *This explains why a man leaves his father and mother and is joined to his wife, and the two are united into one.*

Gen. 2:24

Since they are no longer two but one, let no one separate them, for God has joined them together."

195

"Then why did Moses say a man could merely write an official letter of divorce and send her away?" they asked.

I replied, "Moses wrote those instructions only as a concession to your hard-hearted wickedness, but it was not what God had originally intended."

Later, when I was alone with my disciples in the house, they brought up the subject again. I told them, "Whoever divorces his wife and marries another commits adultery against her—unless his wife has been unfaithful." If a woman divorces her husband and remarries, she commits adultery. And anyone who marries a divorced woman commits adultery."

My disciples then said to me, "Then it is better not to marry!"

"Not everyone can accept this statement," I said. "Only those whom God helps. Some are born as eunuchs, some have been made that way by others, and some choose not to marry for the sake of the Kingdom of Heaven. Let anyone who can, accept this statement."

Mt. 13:53a, 19:1-12; Mk. 10:1b-12; Lu. 16:18

I Blessed the Children

One day some parents brought their children to me so I could lay my hands on them and pray for them, but the disciples told them not to bother me. But when I saw what was happening, I was very displeased with my disciples. I called for the children and said to the disciples, "Let the children come to me. Don't stop them! For the Kingdom of God belongs to such as these. I assure you, anyone who doesn't have their kind of faith will never get into the Kingdom of God." Then I took the children into my arms and placed my hands on their heads and blessed them before I left.

Mt. 19:13-15; Mk. 10:13-16; Lu. 18:15-17

The Disadvantage of Riches

As I was starting out on a trip, a man came running up to me, knelt down, and asked, "Good Teacher, what should I do to get eternal life?"

"Why do you ask me about what is good? Only God truly is good. But to answer your question, you can receive eternal life if you keep the commandments."

"Which ones?" the man asked. And I replied:

Do not murder. Do not commit adultery. Do not steal.
Do not testify falsely. Do not cheat. Honor your father
and mother. Love your neighbor as yourself.

Exodus 20:12-16; Lev. 19:18; Deut. 5:16-20

"Teacher," the man replied, "I've obeyed all these commandments since I was a child. What else must I do?"

I felt genuine love for this man as I looked at him. "There is still one thing you lack," I told him. "If you want to be perfect, go and sell all you have and give the money to the poor, and you will have treasure in heaven. Then come, follow me." But when the young man heard this, his face fell, and he went sadly away because he was very rich. He had many possessions.

I watched him go, then looked around and said to my disciples, "I tell you the truth, it is very hard for rich people to get into the Kingdom of God!" This amazed them. But I said again, "Dear children, it is very hard to get into the Kingdom of God. I say it again—it is easier for a camel to go through the eye of a needle than for a rich person to enter the Kingdom of God."

The disciples were astounded. "Then who in the world can be saved?" they asked. I looked at them intently and said, "Humanly speaking, it is impossible. But not with God. Everything is possible with God."

Mt. 19:16-26; Mk. 10:17-27; Lu. 18:18-27

The Consequences of Following Me

Then Peter began to mention all that he and the other disciples had left behind. Peter said, "We've left our homes and given up everything to follow you. What will we get out of it?" And I replied, "I assure you that when I, the Son of Man, sit upon my glorious throne in the Kingdom, you who have been my followers will also sit on twelve thrones, judging the twelve tribes of Israel.

"And everyone who has given up houses or brothers or sisters or father or mother or wife or children or property, for my sake and for the Good News, will receive a hundred times as much in return in this life—with persecutions—as well as receiving eternal life in the world to come. But many who seem to be important now will be the least important then, and those who are considered least here will be the greatest then.

"For the Kingdom of Heaven is like the owner of an estate who

of the day.

"At noon and again around three o'clock he did the same thing. At five o'clock that evening he was in town again and saw some more people standing around. He asked them, 'Why haven't you been working today?' They replied, 'Because no one hired us.' The owner of the estate told them, 'Then go on out and join the others in my vineyard.'

"That evening he told the foreman to call the workers in and pay them, beginning with the last workers first. When those hired at five o'clock were paid, each received a full day's wage. When those hired earlier came to get their pay, they assumed they would receive more. But they, too, were paid a day's wages. When they received their pay, they protested, 'Those people worked only one hour, and yet you've paid them as much as you paid us who worked all day in the scorching heat.'

"He answered one of them, 'Friend, I haven't been unfair! Didn't you agree to work all day for the usual wage? Take it and go. I wanted to pay this last worker the same as you. Is it against the law for me to do what I want with my money? Should you be angry because I am kind?'

"And so it is, that many who are first now will be last then; and those who are last now will be first then."

Mt. 19:27-20:16; Mk. 10:28-31; Lu. 18:28-30

I Spoke Words of Wisdom to My Disciples

Meanwhile, the crowds grew until thousands were milling about and crushing each other. I turned first to my disciples and warned them, "Beware of the yeast of the Pharisees—beware of their hypocrisy. The time is coming when everything will be revealed; all that is secret will be made public. Whatever you have said in the dark will be heard in the light, and what you have whispered behind closed doors will be shouted from the housetops for all to hear!

"Dear friends, don't be afraid of those who want to kill you. They can only kill the body; they cannot do any more to you. But I'll tell you whom to fear. Fear God, who has the power to kill people and then throw them into hell.

"What is the price of five sparrows? A couple of pennies? Yet God does not forget a single one of them. And the very hairs on your head are all numbered. So don't be afraid; you are more valuable to him than a whole flock of sparrows.

"And I assure you of this: If anyone acknowledges me publicly here on earth, I, the Son of Man, will openly acknowledge that person in the presence of God's angels. But if anyone denies me here on earth, I will deny that person before God's angels. Yet those who

198

speak against the Son of Man may be forgiven, but anyone who speaks blasphemies against the Holy Spirit will never be forgiven.

"And when you are brought to trial in the synagogues and before rulers and authorities, don't worry about what you say in your defense, for the Holy Spirit will teach you what needs to be said even as you are standing there."

The greedy man with large barns

Then someone called from the crowd, "Teacher, please tell my brother to divide our father's estate with me." I replied, "Friend, who made me a judge over you to decide such things as that?"

Then I said, "Beware! Don't be greedy for what you don't have. Real life is not measured by how much you own." And I gave an illustration:

"A rich man had a fertile farm that produced fine crops. In fact, his barns were full to overflowing. So he said, 'I know! I'll tear down my barns and build bigger ones. Then I'll have room enough to store everything. And I'll sit back and say to myself, my friend, you have enough stored away for years to come. Now take it easy! Eat, drink, and be merry!' But God said to him, 'You fool! You will die this very night. Then who will get it all?' Yes, a person is a fool to store up earthly wealth but not have a rich relationship with God."

Learn from the ravens and lilies

Then turning to my disciples, I said, "So I tell you, don't worry about everyday life—whether you have enough food to eat or clothes to wear. For life consists of far more than food and clothing. Look at the ravens. They don't need to plant or harvest or put food in barns because God feeds them. And you are far more valuable to him than any birds! Can all your worries add a single moment to your life? Of course not! And if worry can't do little things like that, what's the use of worrying over bigger things?

"Look at the lilies and how they grow. They don't work or make their clothing, yet Solomon in all his glory was not dressed as beautifully as they are. And if God cares so wonderfully for flowers that are here today and gone tomorrow, won't he more surely care for you? You have so little faith! And don't worry about food—what to eat and drink. Don't worry whether God will provide it for you. These things dominate the thoughts of most people,* but your Father already knows your needs. He will give you all you need from day to day if you make the Kingdom of God your primary concern.

"So don't be afraid, little flock. For it gives your Father great happiness to give you the Kingdom."

199

Prepare for the master's return

"Sell what you have and give to those in need. This will store up treasures for you in heaven! And the purses of heaven have no holes in them. Your treasure will be safe—no thief can steal it and no moth can destroy it. Wherever your treasure is, there your heart will also be.

"Be dressed for service and well prepared, as though you were waiting for your master to return from the wedding feast. Then you will be ready to open the door and let him in the moment he arrives and knocks. There will be special favor for those who are ready and waiting for his return. I tell you, he himself will seat them, put on an apron, and serve them as they sit and eat! He may come in the middle of the night or just before dawn. But whenever he comes, there will be special favor for his servants who are ready!"

The homeowner and the burglar

"Know this: A homeowner who knew exactly when a burglar was coming would not permit the house to be broken into. You must be ready all the time, for the Son of Man will come when least expected."

The master and his servants

Peter asked, "Lord, is this illustration just for us or for everyone?"

And I replied, "I'm talking to any faithful, sensible servant to whom the master gives the responsibility of managing his household and feeding his family. If the master returns and finds that the servant has done a good job, there will be a reward. I assure you, the master will put that servant in charge of all he owns. But if the servant thinks, 'My master won't be back for awhile,' and begins oppressing the other servants, partying, and getting drunk—well, the master will return unannounced and unexpected. He will tear the servant apart and banish him with the unfaithful. The servant will be severely punished, for though he knew his duty, he refused to do it.

"But people who are not aware that they are doing wrong will be punished only lightly. Much is required from those to whom much is given, and much more is required from those to whom more is given."

I bring division

"I have come to bring fire to the earth, and I wish that my task were already completed! There is a terrible baptism ahead of me, and I am under a heavy burden until it is accomplished. Do you think I have come to bring peace to the earth? No, I have come to bring strife and division! From now on families will be split apart, three in favor of me, and two against—or the other way around. There will be a division between father and son, mother and daughter, mother-in-law and daughter-in-law."

Understanding the signs of the time

Then I turned to the crowd and said, "When you see clouds beginning to form in the west, you say, 'Here comes a shower.' And you are right. When the south wind blows, you say, 'Today will be a scorcher.' And it is. You hypocrites! You know how to interpret the appearance of the earth and the sky, but you can't interpret these present times.

"Why can't you decide for yourselves what is right? If you are on the way to court and you meet your accuser, try to settle the matter before it reaches the judge, or you may be sentenced and handed over to an officer and thrown in jail. And if that happens, you won't be free again until you have paid the last penny."

This is the time to repent

About this time I was informed that Pilate had murdered some people from Galilee as they were sacrificing at the Temple in Jerusalem. "Do you think those Galileans were worse sinners than other people from Galilee?" I asked. "Is that why they suffered? Not at all! And you will also perish unless you turn from your evil ways and turn to God. And what about the eighteen men who died when the Tower of Siloam fell on them? Were they the worst sinners in Jerusalem? No, and I tell you again that unless you repent, you will also perish."

Then I used this illustration:

The fruitless fig tree

A man planted a fig tree in his garden and came again and again to see if there was any fruit on it, but he was always disappointed. Finally, he said to his gardener, 'I've waited three years, and there hasn't been a single fig! Cut it down. It's taking up space we can use for something else.' The gardener answered, 'Give it one more chance. Leave it another year, and I'll give it special attention and plenty of fertilizer. If we get figs next year, fine. If not, you can cut it down.'"

Lu. 12:1-13:9

Again, I Healed on the Sabbath

One Sabbath day as I was teaching in a synagogue, I saw a woman who had been crippled by an evil spirit. She had been bent double for eighteen years and was unable to stand up straight. When I saw her, I called her over and said, "Woman, you are healed of your sickness!" Then I touched her, and instantly she could stand straight. How she praised and thanked God!

But the leader in charge of the synagogue was indignant that I had healed her on the Sabbath Day. "There are six days of the week for working," he said to the crowd. "Come on those days to be healed, not on the Sabbath."

But I replied, "You hypocrite! You work on the Sabbath Day! Don't you untie your ox or your donkey from their stalls on the Sabbath and lead them out for water? Wasn't it necessary for me, even on the Sabbath day, to free this dear woman from the bondage in which Satan has held her for eighteen years?"

This shamed my enemies. And all the people rejoiced at the wonderful things I did.

Then I said, "What is the Kingdom of God like? How can I illustrate it? It is like a tiny mustard seed planted in a garden; it grows and becomes a tree, and the birds come and find shelter among its branches."

I also asked, "What else is the Kingdom of God like? It is like yeast used by a woman making bread. Even though she used a large amount of flour, the yeast permeated every part of the dough."

Lu. 13:10-21

I
PRESSED ON
TOWARD
JERUSALEM

chance. Leave it another year, and I'll give it special attention and plenty of fertilizer. If we get figs next year, fine. If not, you can cut it down.'"

Lu. 12:1-13:9

Again, I Healed on the Sabbath

One Sabbath day as I was teaching in a synagogue, I saw a woman who had been crippled by an evil spirit. She had been bent double for eighteen years and was unable to stand up straight. When I saw her, I called her over and said, "Woman, you are healed of your sickness!" Then I touched her, and instantly she could stand straight. How she praised and thanked God!

But the leader in charge of the synagogue was indignant that I had healed her on the Sabbath Day. "There are six days of the week for working," he said to the crowd. "Come on those days to be healed, not on the Sabbath."

But I replied, "You hypocrite! You work on the Sabbath Day! Don't you untie your ox or your donkey from their stalls on the Sabbath and lead them out for water? Wasn't it necessary for me, even on the Sabbath day, to free this dear woman from the bondage in which Satan has held her for eighteen years?"

This shamed my enemies. And all the people rejoiced at the wonderful things I did.

Then I said, "What is the Kingdom of God like? How can I illustrate it? It is like a tiny mustard seed planted in a garden; it grows and becomes a tree, and the birds come and find shelter among its branches."

I also asked, "What else is the Kingdom of God like? It is like yeast used by a woman making bread. Even though she used a large amount of flour, the yeast permeated every part of the dough."

Lu. 13:10-21

I Continued on Toward Jerusalem; My Disciples Were Filled with Dread

March   AD 30

I went through the towns and villages, teaching as I went, always pressing on toward Jerusalem.

Someone asked me, "Lord, will only a few be saved?"

I replied, "The door of heaven is narrow. Work hard to get in, because many will try to enter, but when the head of the house has locked the door, it will be too late. Then you will stand outside knocking and pleading, 'Lord, open the door for us!' But he will reply, 'I do not know you.' You will say, 'But we ate and drank with you, and you taught in our streets.' And he will reply, 'I tell you, I don't know you. Go away, all you who do evil.'

"And there will be great weeping and gnashing of teeth, for you will see Abraham, Isaac, Jacob, and all the prophets within the Kingdom of God, but you will be thrown out. Then people will come from all over the world to take their places in the Kingdom of God. And note this: Some who are despised now will be greatly honored then; and some who are greatly honored now will be despised then."

A few minutes later some of the Pharisees said to me, "Get out of here if you want to live, because Herod Antipas wants to kill you!" I replied, "Go tell that fox that I will keep on casting out demons and doing miracles of healing today and tomorrow; and the third day I will accomplish my purpose. Yes, today, tomorrow, and the next day I must proceed on my way. For it wouldn't do for a prophet of God to be killed except in Jerusalem!

"O Jerusalem, Jerusalem, the city that kills the prophets and stones God's messengers! How often I have wanted to gather your children together as a hen protects her chicks beneath her wings, but you wouldn't let me. And now look, your house is left to you, empty and desolate. For I tell you this, you will never see me again until you say,

Bless the one who comes in the name of the Lord!

Ps. 118:6

We were now on our way to Jerusalem and I was walking ahead of them.

The disciples were filled with dread and the people following behind were overwhelmed with fear. Taking the twelve disciples aside privately, I once more began to describe everything that was about to happen to me. "As you know, we are going to Jerusalem,"

I told them. "And when we get there, all the predictions of the ancient prophets concerning the Son of Man will come true. He will be betrayed to the leading priests and the teachers of the religious law. They will sentence him to die. Then they will hand him over to the Romans to be mocked, treated shamefully, and spit upon. They will whip him and kill him, but on the third day he will rise again from the dead."

But they didn't understand a thing I said. Its significance was hidden from them, and they failed to grasp what I was talking about.

Mt. 20:17-19, 23:37-39; Mk. 10:32-34; Lu. 13:22-35,18:31-34

James and John Made a Request

Then the mother of James and John, the sons of Zebedee, came to me with her sons. She knelt respectfully to ask, "Teacher, we want you to do us a favor."

"What is your request?" I asked. She replied, "In your glorious Kingdom, will you let my two sons sit in places of honor next to you, one at your right and the other at your left?"

But I answered them, "You don't know what you are asking! Are you able to drink from the bitter cup of sorrow I am about to drink? Are you able to be baptized with the baptism of suffering I must be baptized with?"

"Oh yes," they replied, "we are able!"

I told them, "You will indeed drink from my cup and be baptized with my baptism, but I have no right to say who will sit on the thrones next to mine. God has prepared those places for the ones he has chosen."

When the ten other disciples heard what James and John asked, they were indignant. So I called them together and said, "You know that in this world kings are tyrants, and officials lord it over the people beneath them. But among you it should be quite different. Whoever wants to be a leader among you must be your servant, and whoever wants to be first must become the slave for all. For even I, the Son of Man, came here not to be served but to serve others, and to give my life as a ransom for many."

Mt. 20:20-28; Mk. 10:35-45

A Blind Man's Sight Was Restored

Late March AD 30 On the way to Jericho

As we approached Jericho, a huge crowd followed behind.

A blind beggar was sitting beside the road. When he heard the noise of the crowd going past, he asked what was happening. They told him that I, Jesus of Nazareth, was going by. When he heard that I was coming that way, he began shouting, "Lord, Son of David, have mercy on me!"

The crowds ahead of me tried to hush the man, but he only shouted louder, "Son of David, have mercy on me!" When I heard him, I stopped and ordered that the man be brought to me. Then I asked the man, "What do you want me to do for you?"

"Lord," he pleaded, "I want to see!"

And I said, "All right, you can see! Your faith has healed you." Instantly the man could see, and he followed me, praising God. And all who saw it praised God, too.

Mt. 20:29b-30; Lu. 18:35-43

My Meeting with Zacchaeus

Jericho

And so I reached Jericho and made my way through the town.

There was a man there named Zacchaeus. He was one of the most influential Jews in the Roman tax-collecting business, and he had become very rich. He tried to get a look at me, but he was too short to see over the crowds. So he ran ahead and climbed a sycamore tree beside the road, so he could watch from there.

When I came by, I looked up at Zacchaeus and called him by name. "Zacchaeus!" I said. "Quick, come down! For I must be a guest in your home today."

Zacchaeus quickly climbed down and took me to his house in great excitement and joy. But the crowds were displeased. "He has gone to be the guest of a notorious sinner," they grumbled.

Meanwhile, Zacchaeus stood there and said to me, "I will give half my wealth to the poor, Lord, and if I have overcharged people on their taxes, I will give them back four times as much!"

I responded, "Salvation has come to this home today, for this man has shown himself to be a son of Abraham. And I, the Son of Man, have come to seek and save those like him who are lost."

Mk. 10:46a; Lu 19:1-10

Another Man Received His Sight

Outside of Jericho

Later, as my disciples and I left town, a great crowd was following.

A blind beggar named Bartimaeus (son of Timaeus) was sitting beside the road as I was going by. When Bartimaeus heard that I,

Jesus from Nazareth, was nearby, he began to shout out, "Jesus, Son of David, have mercy on me!"

"Be quiet!" the crowd of people yelled at him. But he only shouted louder, "Son of David, have mercy on me!"

When I heard him, I stopped on the road and called, "What do you want me to do for you?"

"Teacher," the blind man said, "I want to see."

I felt sorry for him and said, "Tell him to come here." So they called the blind man. "Cheer up," they said. "Come on, he's calling you!" Bartimaeus threw aside his coat, jumped up, and came to me.

I touched his eyes and said, "Go your way. Your faith has healed you." And instantly the blind man could see! Then he followed me down the road.

Mt. 20:29a, 31-34; Mk. 10: 46b-52

I Was Nearing Jerusalem

The crowd was listening to everything I said. And because I was nearing Jerusalem, I told a story to correct the impression that the Kingdom of God would begin right away. I said, "A nobleman was called away to a distant empire to be crowned king and then return. Before he left, he called together ten servants and gave them ten pounds of silver to invest for him while he was gone. But his people hated him and sent a delegation after him to say they did not want him to be their king.

"When he returned, the king called the servants to whom he had given the money. He wanted to find out what they had done with the money and what their profits were. The first servant reported a tremendous gain—ten times as much as the original amount! 'Well done!' the king exclaimed. 'You are a trustworthy servant. You have been faithful with the little I entrusted to you, so you will be governor of ten cities as your reward.'

"The next servant also reported a good gain—five times the original amount. 'Well done!' the king said. 'You can be governor over five cities.'

"But the third servant brought back only the original amount of money and said, 'I hid it and kept it safe. I was afraid because you are a hard man to deal with, taking what isn't yours and harvesting crops you didn't plant.'

"'You wicked servant!' the king roared. 'Hard, am I? If you knew so much about me and how tough I am, why didn't you deposit the money in the bank so I could at least get some interest on it?' Then turning to the others standing nearby, the king ordered, 'Take the money from this servant, and give it to the one who earned the most.'

"'But, master,' he said, 'that servant has enough already!'

'Yes,' the king replied, 'but to those who use well what they are given, even more will be given. But from those who are unfaithful, even what little they have will be taken away. And now about these enemies of mine who didn't want me to be their king—bring them in and execute them right here in my presence.'"

After telling this story, I went on toward Jerusalem, walking ahead of my disciples.

Lu. 19:11-28

"'But, master,' he said, 'that servant has enough already!' 'Yes,' the king replied, 'but to those who use well what they are given, even more will be given. But from those who are unfaithful, even what little they have will be taken away. And now about these enemies of mine who didn't want me to be their king—bring them in and execute them right here in my presence.'"

After telling this story, I went on toward Jerusalem, walking ahead of my disciples.

Lu. 19:11-28

PART VI

MY
FOURTH
AND FINAL
VISIT TO
JERUSALEM
DURING
MY MINISTRY

SPRING, AD 30

THE
FOURTH PASSOVER
(IN JERUSALEM)
SPRING, AD 30

MARCH 30, AD 30

Mary Anointed My Head and Feet

Saturday, March 30, AD 30   Bethany

It was now almost time for the celebration of Passover, and many people from the country arrived in Jerusalem several days early so they could go through the cleansing ceremony before the Passover began. They wanted to see me, and as they talked in the Temple, they asked each other, "What do you think? Will he come for the Passover?" Meanwhile, the leading priests and Pharisees had publicly announced that anyone seeing me must report me immediately so they could arrest me.

Six days before the Passover ceremonies began, I arrived in Bethany, the home of Lazarus—the man I had raised from the dead. A dinner was prepared in my honor at the house of Simon, a man who had leprosy. Martha served, and Lazarus sat at the table with me. During supper, Mary came in with a beautiful twelve-ounce jar of expensive perfume made from essence of nard. She broke the seal and poured the perfume over my head; she anointed my feet with it and wiped my feet with her hair. And the house was filled with fragrance.

The disciples were indignant when they saw this. They said, "What a waste of money." And they scolded her harshly. Judas Iscariot, one of my disciples—the one who would betray me—said, "That perfume was worth a small fortune. It should have been sold and the money given to the poor." Not that he cared for the poor—he was a thief who was in charge of the disciples' funds, and he often took some for his own use.

But I replied, "Leave her alone. She has poured this perfume on me to prepare my body for burial. Why berate her for doing such a good thing to me? You will always have the poor among you, and you can help them whenever you want. But I will not be here with you much longer. She has done what she could and anointed my body for burial ahead of time. I assure you, wherever the Good News is preached throughout the world, this woman's deed will be talked about in her memory."

When all the people heard of my arrival, they flocked to see me and also to see Lazarus, the man I had raised from the dead. Then the leading priests decided to kill Lazarus, too, for it was because of him that many of the people had deserted them and believed in me.

Mt. 26:6-13; Mk. 14:3-9; Jo. 11:55-12:11

MARCH 31, AD 30

THE
CROWDS
GREETED ME
AS I ENTERED
JERUSALEM
MARCH 31, AD 30

I Received Public Acclamation

Sunday, March 31, AD 30   Jerusalem

The next day, news that I was on the way to Jerusalem swept through the city. As my disciples and I approached Jerusalem, we came to the town of Bethphage, on the Mount of Olives.

I sent two of them on ahead. "Go into the village over there," I said, "and as soon as you enter it, you will see a donkey tied there, with a colt beside it that has never been ridden. Untie it and bring it here. If anyone asks what you are doing, just say, 'The Lord needs it and will return it soon.'"

The two disciples left and found the colt, just as I had said, standing in the street, tied outside a house. And sure enough, as they were untying it, the owners demanded, "What are you doing, untying that colt?"

And the disciples simply replied, "The Lord needs it." They said what I had told them to say, and they were permitted to take it. So they brought the colt to me and threw their garments over it, and I sat on it. This was done to fulfill the prophecy,

> *Tell the people of Israel, "Don't be afraid. Look, your King is coming to you. He is humble, riding on a donkey—even on a donkey's colt."*

Isa. 62:11; Zech. 9:9

My disciples didn't realize at the time that this was a fulfillment of prophecy. But after I entered into my glory, they remembered that these Scriptures had come true before their eyes.

As we reached the place where the road started down from the Mount of Olives, all of my followers began to shout and sing as they walked along, praising God for all the wonderful miracles they had seen.

A huge crowd of Passover visitors came down the road to meet me. Many in the crowd spread their coats on the road ahead of me, and others cut leafy palm branches in the fields and spread them along the way.

I was in the center of the procession, and the crowds all around me were shouting,

> *Praise God! Bless the one who comes in the name of the Lord! Hail to the King of Israel! Bless the coming kingdom of our ancestor David! Peace in heaven and glory in the highest heaven. Praise God in highest heaven!*

Ps. 118:24-25, 148:1

But some of the Pharisees among the crowd said, "Teacher, rebuke your followers for saying things like that!"

I replied, "If they kept quiet, the stones along the road would burst into cheers!"

As we came closer to Jerusalem and I saw the city ahead, I began to cry. "I wish that even today you would find the way of peace. But now it is too late, and peace is hidden from you. Before long your enemies will build ramparts against your walls and encircle you and close in on you. They will crush you to the ground, and your children with you. Your enemies will not leave a single stone in place, because you have rejected the opportunity God offered you."

The entire city of Jerusalem was stirred as I entered. "Who is this?" they asked. And the crowds replied, "It's Jesus, the prophet from Nazareth in Galilee."

Those in the crowd who had seen me call Lazarus back to life were telling others about it. That was the main reason so many went out to meet me—because they had heard about this mighty miracle.

Then the Pharisees said to each other, "We've lost. Look, the whole world has gone after him!"

So I came to Jerusalem and went into the Temple. I looked around carefully at everything, and then I left because it was late in the afternoon. Then I went out to Bethany with the twelve disciples, where I stayed overnight.

Mt. 21:1-11; Mk. 11:1-11; Lu.19:29-44; Jo. 12:12-19

APRIL 1, AD 30

I
MINISTERED
IN THE TEMPLE
APRIL 1, AD 30

I Cursed a Fig Tree

April 1, AD 30

The next morning as we were leaving Bethany, I felt hungry.

Returning to Jerusalem, I noticed a fig tree beside the road a little way off that was in full leaf. I went over to it to see if I could find any figs on it. But there were only leaves because it was too early in the season for fruit. Then I said to the tree, "May you never bear fruit and no one ever eat your fruit again!" And the disciples heard me say it.

Mt. 21:18-19a; Mk. 11:12-14

I Cleared the Temple for the Second Time

When we arrived back in Jerusalem, I entered the Temple and began to drive out the merchants and their customers. I knocked over the tables of the money changers and the stalls of those selling doves, and I stopped everyone from bringing in merchandise. I told them, "The Scriptures declare,

> *My Temple will be called a place of prayer for all nations,*
>
> Isa. 56:7; Jer. 7:11

but you have turned it into a den of thieves!"

The blind and the lame came to me, and I healed them there in the Temple. The leading priests, the teachers of religious law, and other leaders saw these wonderful miracles and heard even the little children in the Temple shouting, "Praise God for the Son of David." But they were indignant and asked me, "Do you hear what these children are saying?"

"Yes," I replied. "Haven't you ever read the Scriptures? For they say,

> *You have taught children and infants to give you praise.*
>
> Ps 8:2

That evening the disciples and I left the city. I returned to Bethany where I stayed overnight.

After that I taught daily in the Temple, but the leading priests, the teachers of religious law, and other leaders of the people began planning how to kill me. But they could think of nothing. They were afraid of me because all the people were so enthusiastic about my teaching, they hung on every word I said.

Mt. 21:12-17; Mk. 11:15-19; Lu. 19:45-48

APRIL 2, AD 30

I
RETURNED
TO THE TEMPLE
APRIL 2, AD 30

The Withered Fig Tree

The next morning as we passed by the fig tree I had cursed, the disciples noticed it was withered from the roots.

Peter remembered what I had said to the tree on the previous day and exclaimed, "Look, Teacher! The fig tree you cursed has withered!" The disciples were amazed when they saw this and asked, "How did it wither so quickly?"

Then I said to them, "Have faith in God. I assure you, if you have faith and don't doubt, you can do things like this and much more. You can even say to this mountain, 'May God lift you up and throw you into the sea,' and your command will be obeyed. All that's required is that you really believe and do not doubt in your heart that you will receive what you ask for. Listen to me! You can pray for anything, and if you believe, you will have it. But when you are praying, first forgive anyone you are holding a grudge against, so that your Father in heaven will forgive your sins, too."

Mt. 21:19b-22; Mk. 11:20-26

I Began to Teach in the Temple

By this time we had arrived in Jerusalem again.

As I was walking through the Temple area, teaching and preaching the Good News, the leading priests, the teachers of religious law, and other leaders came up to me. They demanded, "By whose authority did you drive out the merchants from the Temple? Who gave you such authority?"

"I'll tell you who gave me authority to do these things if you answer one question," I replied. "Did John's baptism come from heaven or was it merely human? Answer me!"

They talked it over among themselves. "If we say it was from heaven, he will ask why we didn't believe him. But if we say it was merely human, we'll be mobbed. The people will stone us, because they are convinced he was a prophet."

They were afraid that the people would start a riot, since everyone thought John was a prophet. So they finally replied, "We don't know."

And I responded, "Then I won't answer your question either.

"But what do you think about this? A man with two sons told the older boy, 'Son, go out and work in the vineyard today.' The son answered, 'No, I won't go,' but later he changed his mind and went anyway. Then the father told the other son, 'You go,' and he said,

'Yes, sir, I will.' But he didn't go. Which of the two was obeying his father?"

They replied, "The first, of course."

Then I explained my meaning: "I assure you, corrupt tax collectors and prostitutes will get into the Kingdom of God before you do. For John the Baptist came and showed you the way of life, and you didn't believe him, while tax collectors and prostitutes did. And even when you saw this happening, you refused to turn from your sins and believe him."

Now I turned to the people again and told them this story: "A certain landowner planted a vineyard, built a wall around it, dug a pit for pressing out the grape juice, and built a lookout tower. Then he leased the vineyard to tenant farmers and moved to another country to live for several years.

"At the time of the grape harvest he sent one of his servants to collect his share of the crop. But the farmers grabbed the servant, beat him up, and sent him back empty-handed. The owner then sent another servant, but they beat him over the head and treated him shamefully. The next servant he sent was killed. So the landowner sent a larger group of his servants to collect for him, but the results were the same. Those who were sent were either beaten, stabbed, stoned, killed, or chased away, until there was only one left—his son whom he loved dearly.

"'What will I do?' the owner asked himself. 'I know! I'll send my cherished son.' The owner finally sent him, thinking, 'Surely they will respect my son.'

"But when the farmers saw his son coming, they said to one another, 'Here comes the heir to the estate. Come on, let's kill him and get the estate for ourselves!' So they grabbed him and dragged him out of the vineyard and murdered him.

"When the owner of the vineyard returns," I asked, "what do you suppose he will do to those farmers?"

The religious leaders replied, "He will put the wicked men to a horrible death and lease the vineyard to others who will give him his share of the crop after each harvest."

"But God forbid such a thing should ever happen," my listeners protested.

Then I asked them, "Didn't you ever read this in the Scriptures?

> *The stone rejected by the builders has now become the*
> *cornerstone. This is the Lord's doing, and it is*
> *marvelous to see.*

Ps. 118:22-23

What I mean is that the Kingdom of God will be taken away from you and given to a nation that will produce the proper fruit. Anyone who stumbles over that stone will be broken to pieces, and it will crush anyone on whom it falls."

When the leading priests and Pharisees and teachers of religious law heard me, they realized I was pointing at them—that they were the wicked farmers in my story.

I told them several other stories to illustrate the Kingdom. I said, "The Kingdom of Heaven can be illustrated by the story of a king who prepared a great wedding feast for his son. Many guests were invited, and when the banquet was ready, he sent his servants to notify everyone that it was time to come. But they all refused! So he sent other servants to tell them, 'The feast has been prepared, and choice meats have been cooked. Everything is ready. Hurry! But the guests he had invited ignored them and went about their business, one to his farm, another to his store. Others seized his messengers and treated them shamefully, even killing some of them.

"Then the king became furious. He sent out his army to destroy the murderers and burn their city. And he said to his servants, 'The wedding feast is ready, and the guests I invited aren't worthy of the honor. Now go out to the street corners and invite everyone you see.'

"So the servants brought in everyone they could find, good and bad alike, and the banquet hall was filled with guests. But when the king came in to meet the guests, he noticed a man who wasn't wearing the proper clothes for a wedding. 'Friend,' he asked, 'how is it that you are here without wedding clothes?' And the man had no reply. Then the king said to his aides, 'Bind him hand and foot and throw him out into the outer darkness, where there is weeping and gnashing of teeth. For many are called, but few are chosen.'"

The Jewish leaders wanted to arrest me, but they were afraid to try because the crowds considered me to be a prophet.

Mt. 21:23-22:14; Mk. 11:27-12:12; Lu. 20:1-19

A Plot to Trick Me

Then the Pharisees met together to think of a way to trap me into saying something that could be reported to the Roman governor so he would arrest me. They decided to send some of their disciples, secret agents pretending to be honest men, along with the supporters of Herod, to ask me this question: "Teacher, we know how honest you are. You speak and teach what is right and are not influenced by what others think. You sincerely teach the ways of God regardless of the consequences. You are impartial and don't play favorites. Now tell us what you think about this: Is it right to pay taxes to the Roman government or not? Should we pay them, or should we not?"

But I knew their evil motives. I saw through their trickery and said, "You hypocrites! Whom are you trying to fool with your trick questions? Here, show me a Roman coin used for the tax." When they handed me the coin, I asked, "Whose picture and title are stamped on it?"

"Caesar's," they replied.

"Well, then," I said, "give to Caesar what belongs to him. But everything that belongs to God must be given to God." So they failed to trap me in the presence of the people. Instead, amazed by my answer, they were silenced and went away.

Mt. 22:15-22; Mk. 12:13-17; Lu. 20:20-26

The Sadducees Asked about the Resurrection

That same day some Sadducees stepped forward—a group of Jews who say there is no resurrection after death. They posed this question:

"Teacher, Moses said,

If a man dies without children, his brother should marry the widow and have a child who will be the brother's heir.

Deut. 25:5-6

Well, there were seven brothers. The oldest married and then died without children, so the second brother married the widow. This brother also died without children, and the wife was married to the next brother, and so it went, one after the other, until each of the seven had married her and died, leaving no children. Finally, the woman died, too. So tell us, whose wife will she be in the resurrection? For all seven were married to her?"

I replied, "Your problem is that you don't know the Scriptures, and you don't know the power of God. Marriage is for people here on earth. But that is not the way it will be in the age to come. For those worthy of being raised from the dead won't be married then. And they will never die again. In these respects they are like the angels in heaven. They are children of God raised up to new life. But now, as to whether the dead will be raised—even Moses proved this when he wrote about the burning bush. Haven't you ever read about this in the Scriptures? Long after Abraham, Isaac, and Jacob had died, God said to Moses,

I am the God of Abraham, the God of Isaac, and the God of Jacob.

Exodus 3:6

So he is the God of the living, not the dead. They are all alive to him. You have made a serious error."

238

When the crowds heard me, they were impressed with my teaching. "Well said, Teacher!" remarked some of the teachers of religious law who were standing there. And that ended their questions; no one dared to ask any more.

Mt. 22:23-33; Mk. 12:18-27; Lu. 20:27-40

A Pharisee Asked a Question about the Law

One of the teachers of religious law was standing there listening to the discussion. He realized that I had answered well. But when the Pharisees heard that I had silenced the Sadducees with my reply, they thought up a fresh question of their own to ask me. One of them, an expert in religious law, tried to trap me with this question: "Teacher, of all the commandments, which is the most important commandment in the law of Moses?"

I replied, "The most important commandment is this:

Hear O Israel! The Lord our God is the one and only Lord. And you must love the Lord your God with all your heart, all your soul, all your mind, and all your strength.

Deut. 6:4-5

The second is equally important:

Love your neighbor as yourself.

Lev. 19:18

No other commandment is greater than these. All the other commandments and all the demands of the prophets are based on these two commandments."

The teacher of religious law replied, "Well said, Teacher. You have spoken the truth by saying that there is only one God and no other. And I know it is important to love him with all my heart and all my understanding and all my strength, and to love my neighbor as myself. This is more important than to offer all the burnt offerings and sacrifices required in the law."

Realizing this man's understanding, I said to him, "You are not far from the Kingdom of God." And after that, no one dared to ask me any more questions.

Later, surrounded by the Pharisees as I was teaching the people in the Temple, I asked, "What do you think about the Messiah? Whose son is he?"

They replied, "He is the son of David."

I asked, "Why do the teachers of religious law claim that the Messiah will be the son of David? For David himself, speaking under the inspiration of the Holy Spirit, said,

The Lord said to my Lord, Sit in honor at my right
hand until I humble your enemies beneath your feet.

Since David himself called him Lord, how can he be his son at the same time?"

The crowd listened with interest. No one could answer me. And after that, no one dared to ask me any more questions.

Mt. 22:34-46; Mk. 12:28-37; Lu. 20: 41-44

Beware of Religious Men

Here are some of the other things I taught them at this time. With the crowds listening, I turned to my disciples and said, "Beware of these teachers of religious law! For they love to parade in flowing robes and to have everyone bow to them as they walk in the marketplaces. And how they love the seats of honor in the synagogues and at banquets. But they shamelessly cheat widows out of their property; and then, to cover up the kind of people they really are, they make long prayers in public. Because of this, their punishment will be the greater."

Mk. 12:38-40; Lu. 20:45-47

The Widow's Offering

While I was in the Temple, I went over to the collection box and sat and watched as the crowds dropped in their money. Many rich people put in large amounts. Then a poor widow came and dropped in two pennies. I called my disciples to me and said, "I assure you, this poor widow has given more than all the rest of them. For they have given a tiny part of their surplus; but she, poor as she is, has given everything she has."

Mk. 12:41-44, Lu. 21:1-4

I Denounced Religious Leaders

Then I said to the crowds and to my disciples, "The teachers of religious law and the Pharisees are the official interpreters of the Scriptures. So practice and obey whatever they say to you, but don't follow their example. For they don't practice what they teach. They crush you with impossible religious demands and never lift a finger to help ease the burden.

"Everything they do is for show. On their arms they wear extra wide boxes with Scripture verses inside, and they wear extra long tassels on their robes. And how they love to sit at the head of the table at banquets in the most prominent seats in the synagogue! They enjoy the attention they get on the streets, and they enjoy being called 'Rabbi.' Don't ever let anyone call you 'Rabbi,' for you have only one teacher, and all of you are on the same level as brothers and sisters. And don't address anyone here on earth as 'Father,' for only God in heaven is your spiritual Father. And don't let anyone call you 'Master,' for there is only one master, the Messiah. The greatest among you must be a servant. But those who exalt themselves will be humbled, and those who humble themselves will be exalted.

"How terrible it will be for you teachers of religious law and you Pharisees. Hypocrites! For you won't let others enter the Kingdom of Heaven, and you won't go in. Yes, how terrible it will be for you teachers of religious law and you Pharisees. For you cross land and sea to make one convert, and then you turn him into twice the son of hell as you yourselves are.

"Blind guides! How terrible it will be for you! For you say that it means nothing to swear 'by God's Temple'— you can break that oath. But then you say that it is binding to swear 'by the gold in the Temple.' Blind fools! Which is greater, the gold, or the Temple that makes the gold sacred? And you say that to take an oath 'by the altar' can be broken, but to swear 'by the gifts on the altar' is binding! How blind! For which is greater, the gift on the altar, or the altar that makes the gift sacred? When you swear 'by the altar,' you are swearing by it and by everything on it. And when you swear 'by the Temple,' you are swearing by it and by God who lives in it. And when you swear 'by heaven,' you are swearing by the throne of God and by God, who sits on the throne.

"How terrible it will be for you teachers of religious law and you Pharisees. Hypocrites! For you are careful to tithe even the tiniest part of your income, but you ignore the important things of the law— justice, mercy, and faith. You should tithe, yes, but you should not leave undone the more important things. Blind guides! You strain your water so you won't accidently swallow a gnat; then you swallow a camel!

"How terrible it will be for you teachers of religious law and you Pharisees. Hypocrites! You are careful to clean the outside of the cup and dish, but inside you are filthy—full of greed and self-indulgence! Blind Pharisees! First wash the inside of the cup, and then the outside will become clean, too.

"How terrible it will be for you teachers of religious law and you Pharisees. Hypocrites! You are like whitewashed tombs—beautiful on the outside but filled on the inside with dead people's bones and all sorts of impurity. You try to look like upright people outwardly, but inside your hearts are filled with hypocrisy and lawlessness.

"How terrible it will be for you teachers of religious law and you Pharisees. Hypocrites! For you build tombs for the prophets your ancestors killed and decorate the graves of the godly people your ancestors destroyed. Then you say, 'We never would have joined them in killing the prophets.'

"In saying that, you are accusing yourselves of being the descendants of those who murdered the prophets. Go ahead. Finish what they started. Snakes! Sons of vipers! How will you escape the judgment of hell? I will send you prophets and wise men and teachers of religious law. You will kill some by crucifixion and whip others in your synagogues, chasing them from city to city. As a result, you will become guilty of murdering all the godly people from righteous Abel to Zechariah son of Barachiah, whom you murdered in the Temple between the altar and the sanctuary. I assure you, all the accumulated judgment of the centuries will break upon the heads of this very generation."

Mt. 23:1-36

I
SPOKE PRIVATELY
TO MY
DISCIPLES
APRIL 2, AD 30

I Again Spoke of My Impending Death

Late afternoon

Some Greeks who had come to Jerusalem to attend the Passover paid a visit to Philip, who was from Bethsaida in Galilee. They said, "Sir, we want to meet Jesus." Philip told Andrew about it, and they came together to ask me.

I replied, "The time has come for the Son of Man to enter into his glory. The truth is, a kernel of wheat must be planted in the soil. Unless it dies it will be alone—a single seed. But its death will produce many new kernels—a plentiful harvest of new lives. He who loves his life in this world will lose it. He who despises his life in this world will keep it for eternal life. All those who want to be my disciples must come and follow me, because my servants must be where I am. And if they follow me, the Father will honor them. Now my soul is deeply troubled. Should I pray, 'Father, save me from what lies ahead'? But that is the very reason why I came! Father, bring glory to your name."

Then a voice spoke from heaven, saying, "I have already brought it glory, and I will do it again." When the crowd heard the voice, some thought it was thunder, while others declared an angel had spoken to me.

Then I told them, "The voice was for your benefit, not mine. The time of judgment for the world has come, when the prince of this world will be cast out. And when I am lifted up on the cross, I will draw everyone to myself." I said this to indicate how I was going to die.

"Die?" asked the crowd. "We understood from Scripture that the Messiah would live forever. Why are you saying the Son of Man will die? Who is this Son of Man you are talking about?"

I replied, "My light will shine out for you just a little while longer. Walk in it while you can, so you will not stumble when the darkness falls. If you walk in the darkness, you cannot see where you are going. Believe in the light while there is still time; then you will become children of the light." After saying these things, I went away and was hidden from them.

But despite all the miraculous signs I had done, most of the people did not believe in me. This is exactly what Isaiah the prophet had predicted:

Lord, who has believed our message? To whom will the Lord reveal his saving power?

Isa. 53:1

245

But the people couldn't believe, for as Isaiah also said,

The Lord has blinded their eyes and hardened their hearts—so their eyes cannot see, and their hearts cannot understand, and they cannot turn to me and let me heal them.

Isa. 6:10

Isaiah was referring to me when he made this prediction, because he was given a vision of the Messiah's glory. Many people, including some of the Jewish leaders, believed in me. But they wouldn't admit it to anyone because of their fear that the Pharisees would expel them from the synagogue. For they loved human praise more than the praise of God.

I shouted to the crowds, "If you trust me, you are really trusting God who sent me. For when you see me, you are seeing the one who sent me. I have come as a light to shine in this dark world, so that all who put their trust in me will no longer remain in darkness. If anyone hears me and doesn't obey me, I am not his judge—for I have come to save the world and not to judge it. But all who reject me and my message will be judged at the day of judgment by the truth I have spoken. I don't speak on my own authority. The Father who sent me gave me his own instructions as to what I should say. And I know his instructions lead to eternal life; so I say whatever the Father tells me to say!"

Jo. 12:20-50

I Revealed the Future to My Disciples

The evening of April 2, AD 30

As I was leaving the Temple grounds that day, some of my disciples began talking about the beautiful stonework of the Temple and the memorial decorations on the walls.

One of the disciples pointed out to me the various Temple buildings and said, "Teacher, look at these tremendous buildings! Look at the massive stones in the walls!" But I replied, "Do you see all these buildings? I assure you, the time is coming when all these things will be so completely demolished that not one stone will be left on top of another!"

Later, I sat on the slopes of the Mount of Olives across the valley from the Temple. Peter, James, John, and Andrew came to me privately and asked me, "Teacher, when will all this take place? And will there be any sign ahead of time to signal your return and the end of the world, to show us when all this will be fulfilled?"

I told them, "Don't let anyone mislead you. For many will come in my name, claiming to be the Messiah and saying, 'The time has come!' But don't believe them. They will lead many astray. And wars will break out near and far. And when you hear of wars and insurrections, don't panic. Yes, these things must come, but the end won't follow immediately."

Then I added, "Nations and kingdoms will proclaim war against each other, and there will be great earthquakes in many parts of the world, and famines and epidemics in many lands, and there will be terrifying things and great miraculous signs in the heavens. But all this will be only the beginning of the horrors to come. When these things begin to happen, watch out!

"But before all this occurs, there will be a time of great persecution. You will be handed over to the courts and beaten in the synagogues and prisons. You will be accused before kings and governors of being my followers. This will be your opportunity to tell them about me. So don't worry about how to answer the charges against you, for I will give you the right words and such wisdom that none of your opponents will be able to reply!

"You will be hated all over the world because of your allegiance to me. Even those closest to you—your parents, brothers, relatives, and friends—will betray you. You will be persecuted, arrested, and killed. But when you are arrested and stand trial, don't worry about what to say in your defense. Just say what God tells you to. Then it is not you who will be speaking, but the Holy Spirit. But not a hair on your head will perish! By standing firm, you will win your souls.

"Brother will betray brother to death, fathers will betray their own children, and children will rise against their parents and cause them to be killed. And many false prophets will appear and will lead many people astray. Sin will be rampant everywhere, and the love of many will grow cold. And many will turn from me and betray and hate each other. But those who endure to the end will be saved. And the Good News about the Kingdom will be preached throughout the whole world, so that all nations will hear it; and then, finally, the end will come.

"The time will come when you will see what Daniel the prophet spoke about: the sacrilegious object that causes desecration standing in the holy place where it should not be—reader pay attention! And when you see Jerusalem surrounded by armies, then you will know that the time of destruction has arrived. Then those in Judea must flee to the hills. Let those in Jerusalem escape, and those outside the city should not enter it for shelter. A person outside the house must not go inside to pack. A person in the field must not return even to get a coat. For those will be days of God's vengeance, and the prophetic words of the Scriptures will be fulfilled.

"How terrible it will be for pregnant women and for mothers nursing their babies in those days. And pray that your flight will not be in winter or on the Sabbath. For that will be a time of greater horror than anything the world has ever seen or will ever see again. In fact, unless that time of calamity is shortened, the entire human race will be destroyed. But it will be shortened for the sake of God's chosen ones.

"There will be great distress in the land and wrath upon this people. They will be brutally killed by the sword or sent away as captives to all nations of the world. And Jerusalem will be conquered and trampled down by the Gentiles until the age of the Gentiles comes to an end.

"Then if anyone tells you, 'Look, here is the Messiah' or 'There he is,' don't pay any attention. For the false messiahs and false prophets will rise up and perform great miraculous signs and wonders so as to deceive, if possible, even God's chosen ones. So if anyone tells you, 'Look, the Messiah is out in the desert,' don't bother to go and look. Or 'Look, he is hiding here,' don't believe it! Watch out! I have warned you!

"After those terrible events, at that time, there will be strange events in the skies—signs in the sun, moon, and stars. For as the lightening lights up the entire sky, so it will be when the Son of Man comes. Just as the gathering of vultures shows there is a carcass nearby, so these signs indicate that the end is near. Immediately after those horrible days end, the sun will be darkened, the moon will not give light, the stars will fall from the sky, and the powers of heaven will be shaken.

"And down here on earth the nations will be in turmoil, perplexed by the roaring seas and strange tides. The courage of many people will falter because of the fearful fate they see coming upon the earth, because the stability of the very heavens will be broken up.

"And then at last, the sign of the coming of the Son of Man will appear in the heavens, and there will be deep mourning among all the nations of the earth. And everyone will see the Son of Man arrive on the clouds with great power and glory. And he will send forth his angels with the sound of a mighty trumpet blast to gather together his chosen ones from all over the world—from the farthest ends of the earth and heaven. So when all these things begin to happen, stand straight and look up, for your salvation is near!

"Now learn a lesson from the fig tree, or any other tree. When its buds become tender and its leaves begin to come out, you know without being told that summer is near. Just so, when you see the events I've described beginning to take place, you can know his return is very near, right at the door. You can be sure that the Kingdom of God is near. I assure you, this generation will not pass from the scene before all these things take place. Heaven and earth will disappear, but my words will remain forever.

"However, no one knows the day or the hour when these things will happen, not even the angels in heaven or the Son himself. Only the Father knows. And since you don't know when they will happen, stay alert and keep watch.

"Watch out! Don't let me find you living in careless ease and drunkenness, and filled with the worries of this life. Don't let that day catch you unaware, as in a trap. For that day will come upon everyone living on the earth. Keep a constant watch. And pray that, if possible, you may escape these horrors and stand before the Son of Man.

"When the Son of Man returns, it will be like it was in Noah's day. In those days before the Flood, the people were enjoying banquets and parties and weddings right up to the time Noah entered his boat. People didn't realize what was going to happen until the Flood came and swept them all away. That is the way it will be when the Son of Man comes.

"Two men will be working together in the field; one will be taken, the other left. Two women will be grinding flour at the mill; one will be taken, the other left. So be prepared, because you don't know what day your Lord is coming.

"Know this: A homeowner who knew exactly when a burglar was coming would stay alert and not permit the house to be broken into. You also must be ready all the time. For the Son of Man will come when least expected.

"The coming of the Son of Man can be compared with that of a man who left home to go on a trip. He gave each of his employees instructions about the work they were to do, and he told the gatekeeper to watch for his return. So keep a sharp lookout! For you do not know when the homeowner will return—at evening, midnight, early dawn, or late daybreak. Don't let him find you sleeping when he arrives without warning. What I say to you I say to everyone: Watch for his return!

"Who is a faithful, sensible servant, to whom the master can give the responsibility of managing his household and feeding his family? If the master returns and finds that the servant has done a good job, there will be a reward. I assure you, the master will put that servant in charge of all he owns. But if the servant is evil and thinks, 'My master won't be back for a while,' and begins oppressing the other servants, partying, and getting drunk—well, the master will return unannounced and unexpected. He will tear the servant apart and banish him with the hypocrites. In that place there will be weeping and gnashing of teeth."

Everyday I went to the Temple to teach, and each evening I returned to spend the night on the Mount of Olives. The crowds gathered early each morning to hear me.

Mt. 24:1-51, Mk. 13:1-37, Lu. 21:5-38

My Final Words about the Kingdom

"The Kingdom of Heaven can be illustrated by the story of ten bridesmaids who took their lamps and went to meet the bridegroom. Five of them were foolish, and five were wise. The five who were foolish took no oil for their lamps, but the other five were wise enough to take along extra oil. When the bridegroom was delayed, they all lay down and slept. At midnight they were roused by the shout, 'Look, the bridegroom is coming! Come and welcome him!'

"All the bridesmaids got up and prepared their lamps. Then the five foolish ones asked the others, 'Please give us some of your oil because our lamps are going out.' But the others replied, 'We don't have enough for all of us. Go to a shop and buy some for yourselves.'

"But while they were gone to buy oil, the bridegroom came, and those who were ready went in with him to the marriage feast, and the door was locked. Later, when the other five bridesmaids returned, they stood outside, calling, 'Sir, open the door for us!' But he called back, 'I don't know you!'

"So stay awake and be prepared, because you do not know the day or the hour of my return.

"Again, the Kingdom of Heaven can be illustrated by the story of a man going on a trip. He called together his servants and gave them money to invest for him while he was gone. He gave five bags of gold to one, two bags of gold to another, and one bag of gold to the last—dividing it in proportion to their abilities—and then left on his trip. The servant who received the five bags of gold began immediately to invest the money and soon doubled it. The servant with the two bags of gold also went right out to work and doubled the money. But the servant who received the one bag of gold dug a hole in the ground and hid the master's money for safekeeping.

"After a long time their master returned from his trip and called them to give an account of how they had used his money. The servant to whom he had entrusted the five bags of gold said, 'Sir, you gave me five bags of gold to invest, and I have doubled the amount.' The master was full of praise. 'Well done, my good and faithful servant. You have been faithful in handling this small amount, so now I will give you many more responsibilities. Let's celebrate together!'

"Next came the servant who had received the two bags of gold with the report, 'Sir, you gave me two bags of gold to invest, and I

250

have doubled the amount.' The master said, 'Well done, my good and faithful servant. You have been faithful in handling this small amount, so now I will give you many more responsibilities. Let's celebrate together!'

"Then the servant with the one bag of gold came and said, 'Sir, I know you are a hard man, harvesting crops you didn't cultivate. I was afraid I would lose your money, so I hid it in the earth and here it is.'

"But the master replied, 'You wicked and lazy servant! You think I'm a hard man, do you, harvesting crops I didn't plant and gathering crops I didn't cultivate? Well, you should at least have put my money into the bank so I could have some interest. Take the money from this servant and give it to the one with the ten bags of gold.

"To those who use well what they are given, even more will be given, and they will have an abundance. But from those who are unfaithful, even what little they have will be taken away. Now throw this useless servant into outer darkness, where there will be weeping and gnashing of teeth.'

"But when the Son of Man comes in his glory, and all the angels with him, then he will sit upon his glorious throne. All the nations will be gathered in his presence, and he will separate them as a shepherd separates the sheep from the goats. He will place the sheep at his right hand and the goats at his left. Then the King will say to those on the right, 'Come, you who are blessed by my Father, inherit the Kingdom prepared for you from the foundation of the world. For I was hungry, and you fed me. I was thirsty, and you gave me a drink. I was a stranger, and you invited me into your home. I was naked, and you gave me clothing. I was sick, and you cared for me. I was in prison, and you visited me.'

"Then these righteous ones will reply, 'Lord, when did we ever see you hungry and feed you? Or thirsty and give you something to drink? Or a stranger and show you hospitality? Or naked and give you clothing? When did we ever see you sick or in prison, and visit you?'

"And the King will tell them, 'I assure you, when you did it to one of the least of these my brothers and sisters, you were doing it to me!'

"Then the King will turn to those on the left and say, 'Away with you, you cursed ones, into the eternal fire prepared for the devil and his demons! For I was hungry, and you didn't feed me. I was thirsty, and you didn't give me anything to drink. I was a stranger, and you didn't invite me into your home. I was naked, and you gave me no clothing. I was sick and in prison, and you didn't visit me.'

"Then they will reply, 'Lord, when did we ever see you hungry and thirsty, or a stranger or naked or sick or in prison, and not help you?'

"And he will answer, 'I assure you, when you refused to help the least of these my brothers and sisters, you were refusing to help me.'

"And they will go away into eternal punishment, but the righteous will go into eternal life."

Mt. 25:1-46

I

WAS BETRAYED
BY JUDAS

APRIL 2, AD 30

Judas Betrayed Me

It was now two days before the Passover celebration and the Festival of Unleavened Bread, which begins the Passover celebration, was drawing near.

When I had finished saying these things, I said to my disciples, "As you know, the Passover celebration begins in two days, and I, the Son of Man, will be betrayed and crucified."

At the same time the leading priests, teachers of religious law, and other leaders were meeting at the residence of Caiaphas, the high priest, actively plotting my murder. They were still looking for an opportunity to capture me secretly and put me to death. "But not during Passover," they agreed, "or there will be a riot"—a possibility they greatly feared.

Then Satan entered into Judas Iscariot, who was one of the twelve disciples, and he went over to the leading priests and captains of the Temple guard to discuss the best way to betray me to them. The leading priests were delighted when they heard why he had come, and they promised him a reward. "How much will you pay me to betray Jesus to you?" Judas asked. And they gave him thirty pieces of silver. From that time on, he began looking for the right time and place to betray me so they could arrest me quietly when the crowds weren't around.

Mt. 26:1-5, 14-16; Mk. 14:1-2, 10-11; Lu. 22:1-6

APRIL 3, AD 30

I
CELEBRATED
THE PASSOVER
FOR
THE
LAST TIME
APRIL 3, AD 30

My Disciples and I Prepared to Eat
the Passover Meal Together

The evening of April 3, AD 30

Now the first day of the Festival of Unleavened Bread arrived, when the Passover lambs were sacrificed.

So I sent Peter and John ahead and said, "Go and prepare the Passover meal, so we can eat together." I sent them into Jerusalem to make the arrangements.

"Where do you want us to go to prepare the supper?" they asked me.

"As soon as you go into the city," I told them, " a man carrying a pitcher of water will meet you. Follow him. At the house he enters, say to the owner, 'The teacher says, My time has come and I will eat the Passover meal at your house. Where is the guest room where I can eat the Passover meal with my disciples?' He will take you upstairs to a large room that is already set up. That is the place; go ahead and prepare our supper there."

The two disciples went on ahead into the city and found everything just as I had said. So they did as I told them and prepared the Passover supper there.

Before the Passover celebration, I knew that my hour had come to leave this world and return to my Father. I now showed the disciples the full extent of my love. It was time for supper, and the devil had already enticed Judas, son of Simon Iscariot, to carry out his plan to betray me.

When it was evening, at the proper time the twelve disciples and I sat down together around the table.

I said, "I have looked forward to this hour with deep longing, anxious to eat this Passover meal with you before my suffering begins. For I tell you now that I won't eat it again until it comes to fulfillment in the Kingdom of God." Then I took a cup of wine, and when I had given thanks for it, I said, "Take this and share it among yourselves. For I will not drink wine again until the Kingdom of God has come."

Mt. 26:17-20; Mk. 14:12-17; Lu. 22:7-18; Jo. 13:1-2

I Washed the Disciples' Feet

I knew that the Father had given me authority over everything and that I had come from God and would return to God. So I got up from the table, took off my robe, wrapped a towel around my waist, and poured water into a basin. Then I began to wash the disciples' feet and to wipe them with the towel I had around me.

When I came to Simon Peter, Peter said to me, "Lord, why are you going to wash my feet?"

I replied, "You don't understand now why I am doing it; someday you will."

"No," Peter protested, "you will never wash my feet."

I replied, "But if I don't wash you, you won't belong to me." Simon Peter exclaimed, "Then wash my hands and head as well, Lord, not just my feet!"

I replied, "A person who has bathed all over does not need to wash, except for the feet, to be entirely clean. And you are clean, but that isn't true of everyone here." For I knew who would betray me. That is what I meant when I said, "Not all of you are clean."

After washing their feet, I put on my robe again and sat down and asked, "Do you understand what I was doing? You call me 'Teacher' and 'Lord,' and you are right, because it is true. And since I, the Lord and Teacher, have washed your feet, you ought to wash each other's feet. I have given you an example to follow. Do as I have done to you. How true it is that a servant is not greater than the master. Nor are messengers more important than the one who sends them. You know these things—now do them! That is the path of blessing.

"I am not saying these things to all of you; I know so well each one of you I chose. The Scriptures declare,

The one who shares my food has turned against me,

Ps. 41:9

and this will soon come true. I tell you this now, so that when it happens you will believe I am the Messiah. Truly, anyone who welcomes my messenger is welcoming me, and anyone who welcomes me is welcoming the Father who sent me."

Jo. 13:3-20

I Told My Disciples that One Will Betray Me and Another Will Deny Knowing Me

Now I was in great anguish of spirit. As we were sitting around the table eating, I said, "The truth is, one of you will betray me." Then the disciples began to ask each other which of them would ever do such a thing. Greatly distressed, one by one they began to ask me, "I'm not the one, am I, Lord?"

I replied, "It is one of you twelve. At this table, sitting here eating among us as a friend, is the man who will betray me. For I, the Son of Man, must die, as the Scriptures declared long ago since it is part of God's plan. But how terrible it will be for my betrayer. Far better for him if he had never been born!"

Judas, the one who would betray me, also asked, "Teacher, I'm not the one, am I?" And I told him, "You have said it yourself."

One of my disciples, the one that I loved, was sitting next to me at the table. Simon Peter motioned to him to ask who would do this terrible thing. Leaning toward me, he asked, "Lord, who is it?"

I said, "It is the one to whom I give the bread dipped in the sauce." And when I had dipped it, I gave it to Judas, son of Simon Iscariot. As soon as Judas had eaten the bread, Satan entered into him. Then I told him, "Hurry. Do it now." None of the others at the table knew what I meant. Since Judas was our treasurer, some thought I was telling him to go and pay for the food or to give some money to the poor. So Judas left at once, going out into the night.

As soon as Judas left the room, I said, "The time has come for me, the Son of Man, to enter into my glory. God will bring me into my glory very soon, and God will receive glory because of all that happens to me."

As we were eating, I took a loaf of bread and asked God's blessing on it. Then I broke it in pieces and gave it to the disciples, saying, "Take it and eat, for this is my body, given for you. Do this in remembrance of me."

After supper I took another cup of wine and gave thanks to God for it. I gave it to them and said, "Each of you drink from it. This wine is a token of God's new covenant to save you, for this is my blood I will pour out for you, which seals the covenant between God and his people. It is poured out to forgive the sins of many. Mark my words—I solemnly declare that I will not drink wine again until the day I drink it new with you in my Father's Kingdom."

And they began to argue among themselves as to who would be the greatest in the coming Kingdom.

I told them, "In this world the kings and great men order their people around, and yet they are called 'friends of the people.' But among you, those who are the greatest should take the lowest rank, and the leader should be like a servant. Normally the master sits at the table and is served by his servants. But not here! For I am your servant. You have remained true to me in my time of trial. And just as my Father has granted me a Kingdom, I now grant you the right to eat and drink at my table in that Kingdom. And you will sit on thrones, judging the twelve tribes of Israel.

"Dear children, how brief are these moments before I must go away and leave you! Then, though you search for me, you cannot come to me—just as I told the Jewish leaders. So now I am giving you a new commandment: Love each other. Just as I have loved you, you should love each other. Your love for one another will prove to the world that you are my disciples."

Simon Peter said, "Lord, where are you going?" And I replied, "You can't go with me now, but you will follow me later."

"But why can't I come now, Lord?" he asked. "I am ready to die for you."

I answered, "Die for me? No, before the rooster crows tomorrow morning, you will deny three times that you even know me.

Mt. 26:21-29; Mk. 14:18-25; Lu. 22:19-30; Jo. 13:21-38

I
ENCOURAGED
MY DISCIPLES
APRIL 3, AD 30

My Promise

"Don't be troubled. You trust God, now trust in me. There are many rooms in my Father's home, and I am going to prepare a place for you. If this were not so, I would tell you plainly. When everything is ready, I will come and get you, so that you will always be with me where I am. And you know where I am going and how to get there."

"No, we don't know, Lord," Thomas said. "We haven't any idea where you are going, so how can we know the way?"

I told him, "I am the way, the truth, and the life. No one can come to the Father except through me. If you had known who I am, then you would have known who my Father is. From now on you know him and have seen him!"

Philip said, "Lord, show us the Father and we will be satisfied."

I replied, "Philip, don't you even yet know who I am, even after all the time I have been with you? Anyone who has seen me has seen the Father! So why are you asking to see him? Don't you believe that I am in the Father and the Father is in me? The words I say are not my own, but my Father who lives in me does his work through me. Just believe that I am in the Father and the Father is in me. Or at least believe because of what you have seen me do.

"The truth is, anyone who believes in me will do the same works I have done, and even greater works, because I am going to be with the Father. You can ask for anything in my name, and I will do it, because the work of the Son brings glory to the Father. Yes, ask anything in my name and I will do it!

"If you love me, you will obey my commandments. And I will ask the Father and he will give you another Counselor, who will never leave you. He is the Holy Spirit, who leads into all truth. The world at large cannot receive him, because it isn't looking for him and doesn't recognize him. But you do, because he lives with you now and later will be in you. No, I will not abandon you as orphans— I will come to you.

"In just a little while the world will not see me again, but you will. For I will live again, and you will, too. When I am raised to life again, you will know that I am in my Father, and you are in me, and I am in you. Those who obey my commandments are the ones who love me. And because they love me, my Father will love them, and I will love them. And I will reveal myself to each one of them."

Judas (not Iscariot, but the other disciple with that name) said to me, "Lord, why are you going to reveal yourself only to us and not to the world at large?"

I replied, "All those who love me will do what I say. My Father will love them, and we will come to them and live with them. Anyone who doesn't love me will not do what I say. And remember, my words are not my own. This message is from the Father who sent me. I am telling you these things now while I am still with you. But when the Father sends the Counselor in my name—and by the Counselor I mean the Holy Spirit—he will teach you everything and will remind you of everything I myself have told you.

"I am leaving you with a gift—peace of mind and heart. And the peace I give isn't like the peace the world gives. So don't be troubled or afraid. Remember what I told you: I am going away, but I will come back to you again. If you really love me, you will be very happy , because now I go to the Father, who is greater than I am. I have told you these things before they happen so that you will believe when they do happen.

"I don't have much more time to talk to you, because the prince of this world approaches. He has no power over me, but I will do what the Father requires of me, so that the world will know that I love the Father. Come, let's be going."

Jo. 14:1-31

I Told My Disciples that I Loved Them

"I am the true vine, and my Father is the gardener. He cuts off every branch that doesn't produce fruit, and he prunes the branches that do bear fruit so they will produce even more. You have already been pruned for greater fruitfulness by the message I have given you. Remain in me, and I will remain in you. For a branch cannot produce fruit if it is severed from the vine, and you cannot be fruitful apart from me.

"Yes, I am the vine; you are the branches. Those who remain in me, and I in them, will produce much fruit. For apart from me you can do nothing. Anyone who parts from me is thrown away like a useless branch and withers. Such branches are gathered into a pile to be burned. But if you stay joined to me and my words remain in you, you may ask any request you like, and it will be granted! My true disciples produce much fruit. This brings great glory to my Father.

"I have loved you even as the Father has loved me. Remain in my love. When you obey me, you remain in my love, just as I obey my Father and remain in his love. I have told you this so that you will be filled with my joy. Yes, your joy will overflow! I command you to love each other in the same way that I love you. And here is how to measure it—the greatest love is shown when people lay down their lives for their friends. You are my friends if you obey me. I no longer call you servants, because a master doesn't confide in his servants. Now you are my friends, since I have told you everything the Father told me. You didn't choose me. I chose you. I appointed you to go and produce fruit that will last, so that the Father will give you whatever you ask for, using my name. I command you to love each other.

"When the world hates you, remember it hated me before it hated you. The world would love you if you belonged to it, but you don't. I chose you to come out of the world, and so it hates you. Do you remember what I told you? 'A servant is not greater than the master.' Since they persecuted me, naturally they will persecute you. And if they had listened to me, they would listen to you! The people of the world will hate you because you belong to me, for they don't know God who sent me. They would not be guilty if I had not come and spoken to them. But now they have no excuse for their sin. Anyone who hates me hates my Father, too. If I hadn't done such miraculous signs among them that no one else could do, they would not be counted guilty. But as it is, they saw all that I did and yet hated both of us—me and my Father. This has fulfilled what the Scriptures said:

They hated me without cause.

Ps. 35:19, 69:4

"But I will send you the Counselor—the Spirit of truth. He will come to you from the Father and will tell you all about me. And you must also tell others about me because you have been with me from the beginning.

"I have told you these things so that you won't fall away. For you will be expelled from the synagogues, and the time is coming when those who kill you will think they are doing God a service. This is because they have never known the Father or me. Yes, I'm telling you these things now, so that when they happen, you will remember I warned you. I didn't tell you earlier because I was going to be with you for a while longer.

"But now I am going away to the one who sent me, and none of you has asked me where I am going. Instead, you are very sad. But it is actually best for you that I go away, because if I don't, the Counselor won't come. If I do go away, he will come because I will send him to you. And when he comes, he will convince the world of its sin, and of God's righteousness, and of the coming judgment. The world's sin is unbelief in me. Righteousness is available because I go to the Father, and you will see me no more. Judgment will come because the prince of this world has already been judged.

"Oh, there is so much more I want to tell you, but you can't bear it now. When the Spirit of truth comes, he will guide you into all truth. He will not be presenting his own ideas; he will be telling you what he has heard. He will tell you about the future. He will bring me glory by revealing to you whatever he receives from me. All that the Father has is mine; this is what I mean when I say that the Spirit will reveal to you whatever he receives from me.

"In just a little while I will be gone, and you won't see me anymore. Then, in just a little while after that, you will see me again."

The disciples asked each other, "What does he mean when he says, 'You won't see me, and then you will see me'? And what does he mean when he says, 'I am going to the Father'? And what does he mean by 'a little while'? We don't understand."

I realized they wanted to ask me, so I said, "Are you asking yourselves what I meant? I said in just a little while I will be gone, and you won't see me anymore. Then, just a little while after that, you will see me again. Truly, you will weep and mourn over what is going to happen to me, but the world will rejoice. You will grieve, but your grief will suddenly turn to wonderful joy when you see me again. It will be like a woman experiencing the pains of labor. When her child is born, her anguish gives place to joy because she has brought a new person into the world. You have sorrow now, but I will see you again; then you will rejoice, and no one can rob you of that joy. At that time you won't need to ask me for anything. The truth is, you can go directly to the Father and ask him, and he will grant your request because you use my name. You haven't done this before. Ask, using my name, and you will receive, and you will have abundant joy.

"I have spoken of these matters in parables, but the time will come when this will not be necessary, and I will tell you plainly all about the Father. Then you will ask in my name. I'm not saying I will ask the Father in your behalf, for the Father himself loves you dearly because you love me and believe that I came from God. Yes, I came from the Father into the world, and I will leave the world and return to the Father."

Then my disciples said, "At last you are speaking plainly and not in parables. Now we understand that you know everything and don't need anyone to tell you anything. From this we believe that you came from God."

I asked, "Do you finally believe? But the time is coming—in fact, it is already here—when you will be scattered, each one going his own way, leaving me alone. Yet I am not alone, because the Father is with me. I have told you all this so that you may have peace in me. Here on earth you will have many trials and sorrows. But take heart, because I have overcome the world."

Jo. 15:1-16:33

270

I
PRAYED
FOR ALL
WHO WOULD
BELIEVE IN ME
APRIL 3, AD 30

I Prayed for All Believers

When I had finished saying all these things, I looked up to heaven and said, "Father, the time has come. Glorify your Son so I can give glory back to you. For you have given me authority over everyone in all the earth. I give eternal life to each one you have given me. And this is the way to have eternal life—to know you, the only true God, and me, the one you sent to earth. I brought glory to you here on earth by doing everything you told me to do. And now, Father, bring me into the glory we shared before the world began.

"I have told these men about you. They were in the world, but then you gave them to me. Actually, they were always yours, and you gave them to me, and they have kept your word. Now they know that everything I have is a gift from you, for I have passed on to them the words you gave me; and they accepted them and know that I came from you, and they believe you sent me.

"My prayer is not for the world, but for those you have given me, because they belong to you. And all of them, since they are mine, belong to you; and you have given them back to me, so they are my glory! Now I am departing the world; I am leaving them behind and coming to you. Holy Father, keep them and care for them—all those you have given me—so that they will be united just as we are. During my time here, I have kept them safe. I guarded them so that not one was lost, except the one headed for destruction as the Scriptures foretold.

"And now I am coming to you. I have told them many things while I was with them so they would be filled with my joy. I have given them your word. And the world hates them because they do not belong to the world, just as I do not. I'm not asking you to take them out of the world, but to keep them safe from the evil one. They are not part of this world any more than I am. Make them pure and holy by teaching them your words of truth. As you sent me into the world, I am sending them into the world. And I give myself entirely to you so they also might be entirely yours.

"I am praying not only for these disciples but also for all who will ever believe in me because of their testimony. My prayer for all of them is that they will be one, just as you and I are one, Father— that just as you are in me and I am in you, so they will be in us, and the world will believe you sent me.

"I have given them the glory you gave me, so that they may be one, as we are—I in them and you in me, all being perfected into one. Then the world will know that you sent me and will understand that you love them as much as you love me. Father, I want these whom you've given me to be with me, so they can see my glory. You gave me the glory because you loved me even before the world began!

"O righteous Father, the world doesn't know you, but I do; and these disciples know you sent me. And I have revealed you to them and will keep on revealing you. I will do this so that your love for me may be in them and I in them."

Jo 17:1-26

I Warned My Disciples

Then I asked them, "When I sent you out to preach the Good News and you did not have money, a traveler's bag, or extra clothing, did you lack anything?"

"No," they replied.

"But now," I said, "take your money and a traveler's bag. And if you don't have a sword, sell your clothes and buy one! For the time has come for this prophecy about me to be fulfilled:

He was counted among those who were rebels.

Isa. 53:12

Yes, everything written about me by the prophets will come true."

"Lord," they replied, "we have two swords among us."

"That's enough," I said.

Then we sang a hymn and, accompanied by the disciples, I left the upstairs room and went as usual to the Mount of Olives.

"Tonight all of you will desert me," I told them. "For the Scriptures say,

God will strike the Shepherd and the sheep of the flock will be scattered.

Zech. 13:7

But after I have been raised from the dead I will go ahead of you to Galilee and meet you there."

Peter declared, "Lord, even if everyone else deserts you, I never will." But I said, "Peter, let me tell you something. The rooster will not crow tomorrow morning until you have denied three times that you even know me."

"Simon, Simon, Satan has asked to have all of you to sift you like wheat. But I pleaded in prayer for you, Simon, that your faith should not fail. So when you have repented and turned to me again, strengthen and build your brothers."

Peter said to me, "Lord, I am ready to go to prison with you, and even to die with you."

"Peter," I replied, "The truth is, this very night, before the rooster crows, you will deny me three times."

"No!" Peter insisted. "Not even if I have to die with you! I will never deny you!" And all the others vowed the same.

Mt. 26:30-35; Mk. 14:26-31; Lu. 22:31-39

THE
DISCIPLES AND I
WENT TO THE
MOUNT OF OLIVES
AT MIDNIGHT
APRIL 3 AD 30

Gethsemane

After saying these things, I crossed the Kidron Valley to the Mount of Olives with my disciples and entered an olive grove called Gethsemane.

There I told them, "Sit here while I go ahead to pray."

I took Peter and Zebedee's two sons, James and John, and I began to be filled with anguish and horror and deep distress. I told them, "My soul is crushed with grief to the point of death. Stay here and watch with me. Pray that you will not be overcome by temptation."

I went on a little farther, about a stone's throw, and knelt and fell face down on the ground. I prayed that, if it were possible, the awful hour awaiting me might pass by me. "Abba, Father," I said, "everything is possible for you. My Father! If you are willing, please take this cup of suffering away from me. Yet I want your will, not mine."

Then I returned to the disciples and found them asleep. I said to Peter, "Simon! Are you asleep? Couldn't you stay awake and watch with me even one hour? Keep alert and pray. Otherwise temptation will overpower you. For though the spirit is willing enough, the body is weak!"

Again I left them and prayed, repeating my pleadings, "My Father! If you are willing, please take this cup away from me. Yet, if this cup cannot be taken away until I drink it, your will be done."

Then an angel from heaven appeared and strengthened me. I prayed more fervently, and was in such agony of spirit that my sweat fell to the ground like great drops of blood.

At last I stood up again and returned to the disciples, only to find them asleep, exhausted from grief, for they just couldn't keep their eyes open. "Why are you sleeping?" I asked. "Get up and pray. Otherwise temptation will overpower you." And they didn't know what to say. So I went back to pray a third time, saying the same things again.

Then I came to my disciples a third time, and said, "Still sleeping? Still resting? Enough! Look, the time has come. I, the Son of Man, am betrayed into the hands of sinners. Up, let's be going. See, my betrayer is here!"

Mt. 26:36-46; Mk. 14:32-42; Lu. 22:40-46; Jo. 18:1

APRIL 4, AD 30

I

WAS

ARRESTED

VERY EARLY

IN THE MORNING

APRIL 4, AD 30

I Was Betrayed with a Kiss

And immediately, even as I said this, a mob that was armed with swords and clubs arrived with Judas, one of my twelve disciples. Judas the betrayer knew this place, because I had gone there many times with my disciples.

The mob had been sent out by the leading priests and Pharisees, the teachers of religious law, and other leaders of the people. The leading priests and Pharisees had given Judas a battalion of Roman soldiers and Temple guards to accompany him. Now with blazing torches, lanterns, and weapons, they arrived at the olive grove.

Judas had given them a prearranged signal: "You will know which one to arrest when I go over and give him the kiss of greeting. Then you can take him away under guard."

As soon as they arrived, Judas came straight over to me. "Greetings, Teacher!" he exclaimed. And I said, "My friend, go ahead and do what you have come for." And he gave me the kiss.

But I said, "Judas, how can you betray me, the Son of Man, with a kiss?"

I fully realized all that was going to happen to me.
Stepping forward to meet them I asked, "Whom are you looking for?"

"Jesus of Nazareth," they replied. "I am he," I said. Judas was standing there with them when I identified myself. And as I said "I am he," they all fell backward to the ground!

Once more I asked them, "Whom are you searching for?" And again they replied, "Jesus of Nazareth."

"I told you that I am he," I said. "And since I am the one you want, let these others go." I did this to fulfill my own statement: "I have not lost a single one of those you gave me."

Then the others grabbed me and arrested me.

When the other disciples saw what was about to happen, they exclaimed, "Lord, should we fight? We brought the swords!" Then Simon Peter pulled out a sword and slashed off the right ear of Malchus, the high priest's servant. But I said, "Don't resist any more." And I touched the place where the man's ear had been and healed him.

And I said to Peter, "Put your sword back into its sheath. Those who use the sword will be killed by the sword. Don't you realize that I could ask my Father for thousands of angels to protect us, and he would send them instantly? But if I did, how would the Scriptures be fulfilled that describe what must happen now? Shall I not drink from the cup the Father has given me?"

Then I said to the crowd, and to the leading priests and captains of the Temple guard and the other leaders who headed the mob,

"Am I some dangerous criminal, that you have come armed with swords and clubs to arrest me? Why didn't you arrest me in the Temple? I was there teaching every day. But this is your moment, the time when the power of darkness reigns. This is all happening to fulfill the words of the prophets as recorded in the Scriptures."

Meanwhile, all the disciples deserted me and fled.

There was a young man following along behind, clothed only in a linen nightshirt. When the mob tried to grab him, they tore off his clothes, but he escaped and ran away naked.

Mt. 26:47-56; Mk. 14:43-52; Lu. 22:47-53; Jo. 18:2-11

I
WAS TRIED
BEFORE THE
ROMAN AND JEWISH
AUTHORITIES
APRIL 4, AD 30

I Was Tried before the Jewish Leaders

efore daybreak, April 4, AD 30   The home of the high priest

So the soldiers, their commanding officer, and the Temple guards arrested me and tied me up. First they took me to the residence of Annas, the father-in-law of Caiaphas, the high priest that year.

Caiaphas was the one who had told the other Jewish leaders, "Better that one should die for all."

Inside, the high priest began asking me about my followers and what I had been teaching them.

I replied, "What I teach is widely known, because I have preached regularly in the synagogues and the Temple. I have been heard by people everywhere, and I teach nothing in private that I have not said in public. Why are you asking me this question? Ask those who heard me. They know what I said."

One of the Temple guards standing there struck me on the face. "Is that the way to answer the high priest?" he demanded.

I replied, "If I said anything wrong, you must give evidence for it. Should you hit a man for telling the truth?"

Then Annas bound me and sent me to the home of Caiaphas, the high priest. The people who arrested me led me to the high priest's residence, where the leading priests, teachers of religious law, and other leaders had gathered.

Simon Peter followed along far behind, as did another of the disciples, and eventually came to the courtyard of the high priest's house. That other disciple was acquainted with the high priest, so he was allowed to enter the courtyard with me. Peter stood outside the gate. Then the other disciple spoke to the woman watching at the gate, and she let Peter in.

The guards and the household servant were standing around a charcoal fire they had made in the courtyard because it was cold. And Peter sat with the guards, warming himself by the fire, and waited to see what was going to happen to me.

Inside, the leading priest and the entire high council were trying to find witnesses who would lie about me, so they could put me to death. But their efforts were in vain. Even though they found many who agreed to give false witness, there was no testimony they could use.

Some men stood up to testify against me, but they contradicted each other. Finally two men were found who declared, "We heard this man say 'I will destroy this Temple of God made with human hands, and in three days I will build another, made without human hands.'" But even then they didn't get their stories straight!

Then the high priest stood up before the others and asked me, "Well, aren't you going to answer these charges? What do you have to say for yourself?" But I made no reply.

Then the high priest asked me, "Are you the Messiah, the Son of the blessed God? I demand in the name of the living God that you tell us whether you are the Messiah, the Son of God."

I replied, "Yes, it is as you say. I am, and in the future you will see me, the Son of Man, sitting at God's right hand in the place of power and coming back on the clouds of heaven."

Then the high priest tore his clothing to show his horror, shouting, "Blasphemy! Why do we need other witnesses? You have all heard his blasphemy. What is your verdict?"

"Guilty!" they shouted. "He must die!" And they all condemned me to death.

Then some of them began to spit at me, and some slapped me in the face. They blindfolded me; then they hit me with their fists. Now the guards in charge of me began mocking and beating me. "Prophesy to us, you Messiah! Who hit you that time, you prophet?" they jeered. The guards threw all sorts of terrible insults at me. And they were hitting me as they led me away.

Mt. 26:57-68; Mk. 14:53-65; Lu. 22:54-55, 63-65; Jo. 18:12-16, 18-24

PETER
DENIED
THAT
HE KNEW ME

Peter Denied Knowing Me

Meanwhile, as Peter was sitting outside in the courtyard warming himself at the fire, a servant girl noticed him in the firelight and began staring at him. She looked closely at him and said, "You were one of those with Jesus the Galilean."

"No," he said, "I am not."

Finally she said, "This man was one of Jesus' followers!"

Peter denied it in front of everyone. "Woman," he said, "I don't know what you're talking about." And he went out into the entryway. Just then, a rooster crowed.

Later, out by the gate, another servant girl noticed him and said to those standing around, "This man was with Jesus of Nazareth. He is definitely one of them!" Someone else looked at him and said, "You must be one of them!" Again, Peter denied it, this time with an oath. "No man, I'm not! I don't even know the man." Peter replied.

About an hour later other bystanders came over to him and said, "You must be one of them; we can tell by your Galilean accent." Someone else insisted, "This must be one of Jesus' disciples because he is a Galilean, too." One of the household servants of the high priest, a relative of the man whose ear Peter had cut off, asked, "Didn't I see you out there in the olive grove with Jesus?" Again Peter denied it. "Man," he said, "I don't know what you're talking about. I swear by God, I don't know the man." And immediately the rooster crowed a second time.

At that moment I turned and looked at Peter.

Suddenly, my words flashed through Peter's mind: "Before the rooster crows twice tomorrow morning you will deny me three times."

And Peter left the courtyard, crying bitterly.

Mt. 26:69-75; Mk. 14:66-72; Lu. 22:56-62; Jo. 18:17, 25-27

I Was Questioned by the High Council

Daybreak, April 4, AD 30

Very early in the morning, at daybreak, the leading priests, other leaders, and teachers of religious law—the entire high council—met again to discuss their next step, how to persuade the Roman government to sentence me to death.

I was led before this high council, and they said, "Tell us if you are the Messiah."

But I replied, "If I tell you, you won't believe me. And if I ask you a question, you won't answer. But the time is soon coming when I, the Son of Man, will be sitting at God's right hand in the place of power."

They all shouted, "Then you claim you are the Son of God?" And I replied, "You are right in saying that I am."

"What need do we have for other witnesses?" they shouted. "We ourselves heard him say it." Then they bound me, and the entire council took me to Pilate, the Roman governor.

Mt. 27:1-2; Mk. 15:1; Lu. 22:66-71

Judas Hanged Himself

When Judas, who had betrayed me, realized that I had been condemned to die, he was filled with remorse. So he took the thirty pieces of silver back to the leading priests and other leaders. "I have sinned," he declared, "for I have betrayed an innocent man."

"What do we care?" they retorted. "That's your problem."

Then Judas threw the money onto the floor of the Temple and went out and hanged himself. The leading priests picked up the money. "We can't put it into the Temple treasury," they said, "since it's against the law to accept money paid for murder."

After some discussion they finally decided to buy the potter's field, and they made it into a cemetery for foreigners. That is why the field is still called the Field of Blood. This fulfilled the prophecy of Jeremiah that says,

They took the thirty pieces of silver—the price at which he was valued by the people of Israel—and purchased the potter's field, as the Lord directed.

Zech. 11:12-13; Jer. 32:6-9

Mt. 27:3-10

I
WAS TRIED
BEFORE THE
ROMAN AND JEWISH
AUTHORITIES
APRIL 4, AD 30

I Was Brought before Pilate and Herod

The morning of April 4, AD 30 Their headquarters

My trial before Caiaphas had ended in the early hours of the morning.

When the entire council took me to the headquarters of the Roman governor to stand before Pilate, my accusers didn't go in themselves. It would defile them, and they wouldn't be allowed to celebrate the Passover feast.

So Pilate, the governor, came out to us and asked, "What is your charge against this man?"

"We wouldn't have handed him over to you if he weren't a criminal!" they retorted.

"Then take him away and judge him by your own laws," Pilate told them.

"Only the Romans are permitted to execute someone," the Jewish leaders replied. This fulfilled my prediction about the way I would die.

They began at once to state their case: "This man has been leading our people to ruin by telling them not to pay their taxes to the Roman government and by claiming that he is a king, the Messiah."

Then Pilate went back inside and called for me to be brought to him. Now I was standing before Pilate, the Roman governor.

"Are you the King of the Jews?" the governor asked me. I replied, "Yes, it is as you say. Is this your own question, or did others tell you about me?"

"Am I a Jew?" Pilate asked. "Your own people and their leading priests brought you here. Why? What have you done?"

Then I answered, "I am not an earthly king. If I were, my followers would have fought when I was arrested by the Jewish leaders. But my Kingdom is not of this world."

Pilate replied, "You are a king then?"

"You say that I am a king, and you are right," I said. "I was born for that purpose. And I came to bring truth to the world. All who love truth recognize that what I say is true."

"What is truth?" Pilate asked. Then he went out again to the people and turned to the leading priests and said, "I find nothing wrong with this man! He is not guilty of any crime."

Then they became desperate. "But he is causing riots everywhere he goes, all over Judea, from Galilee to Jerusalem!"

"Oh, is he a Galilean?" Pilate asked. When they answered that I was, Pilate sent me to Herod Antipas, because Galilee was under Herod's jurisdiction, and Herod happened to be in Jerusalem at the time.

Herod was delighted at the opportunity to see me, because he had heard about me and had been hoping for a long time to see me perform a miracle. He asked me question after question, but I refused to answer.

Meanwhile, the leading priests and the teachers of religious law stood there shouting their accusations. Now Herod and his soldiers began mocking and ridiculing me. Then they put a royal robe on me and sent me back to Pilate.

Herod and Pilate, who had been enemies before, became friends that day.

Pilate called together the leading priests and other religious leaders, along with the people. Then I came out wearing the robe, and he announced his verdict. "You brought this man to me, accusing him of leading a revolt. I have examined him thoroughly on this point in your presence and find him innocent. Herod came to the same conclusion and sent him back to us. Nothing this man has done calls for the death penalty. You have a custom of asking me to release someone from prison each year at Passover. So I will have him flogged, but then I will release him."

Then the leading priests accused me of many crimes, and Pilate asked me, "Don't you hear their many charges against you? Aren't you going to say something?" But I said nothing, much to Pilate's great surprise.

Now, it was the governor's custom to release one prisoner to the crowd each year during the Passover celebration—anyone the people requested. This year there was a notorious criminal in prison, a man named Barabbas who had been convicted along with others for murder and for taking part in an insurrection in Jerusalem against the government.

The mob began to crowd in toward Pilate, asking him to release a prisoner as usual. As the crowds gathered before Pilate's house that morning, he asked them, "Which one do you want me to release to you—Barabbas, or Jesus who is called the Messiah?" (For he realized by now that the leading priests had arrested me out of envy.)

Just then, as Pilate was sitting on the judgement seat, his wife sent him this message: "Leave that innocent man alone, because I had a terrible nightmare about him last night." But at this point the leading priests persuaded the crowds to ask for Barabbas to be released and for me to be put to death.

So when the governor asked again, "Which of these two do you want me to release to you? Should I give you the King of the Jews?" The leading priests and other leaders stirred the mob to demand the release of Barabbas instead of me. The crowd shouted back their reply, "No! Not this man, but Barabbas!" Then a mighty roar rose from the crowd, and with one voice they shouted, "Kill him, and release Barabbas to us!"

Pilate argued with them, because he wanted to release me. "But if I release Barabbas," Pilate asked them, "what should I do with Jesus, this man you call the King of the Jews, the Messiah?" And they all shouted, "Crucify him! Crucify him!"

For the third time he demanded, "Why? What crime has he committed? I have found no reason to sentence him to death. I will therefore flog him and let him go."

And the crowd shouted louder and louder for my death. With one voice the crowd roared. "Crucify him! Away with him," they yelled. "Away with him—crucify him!"

"You crucify him," Pilate said. "I find him not guilty." The Jewish leaders replied, "By our laws he ought to die because he called himself the Son of God."

When Pilate heard this, he was more frightened than ever. He took me back into the headquarters again and asked me, "Where are you from?" But I gave no answer.

"You won't talk to me?" Pilate demanded. "Don't you realize that I have the power to release you or to crucify you?" Then I said, "You would have no power over me at all unless it were given to you from above. So the one who brought me to you has the greater sin."

Then Pilate tried to release me, but the Jewish leaders told him, "If you release this man, you are no friend of Caesar. Anyone who declares himself a king is a rebel against Caesar."

When they said this, Pilate went outside again and said to the people, "I am going to bring him out to you now, but understand clearly that I find him not guilty." Pilate brought me out to them again and said, "Here is the man!" Then Pilate sat down on the judgment seat on the platform that is called the Stone Pavement (in Hebrew, Gabbatha).

When they saw me, the leading priests and Temple guards began shouting, "Crucify! Crucify!"

"What? Crucify your king?" Pilate asked.

"We have no king but Caesar," the leading priests shouted back.

Pilate saw that he wasn't getting anywhere and that a riot was developing. So he sent for a bowl of water and washed his hands before the crowd, saying, "I am innocent of the blood of this man. The responsibility is yours!"

And all the people yelled back. "We will take responsibility for his death—we and our children!"

And their voices prevailed. So Pilate, anxious to please the crowd, delivered me over to them and sentenced me to die as they demanded.

As they requested, he released Barabbas, the man in prison for insurrection and murder. But he turned me over to the Roman soldiers to be crucified.

Some of the governor's soldiers took me into the courtyard of their headquarters, which is called the Praetorium, and called out the entire battalion. They stripped me and put a purple robe on me. They made a crown of long, sharp thorns and put it on my head, and they placed a stick in my right hand as a scepter.

Then they saluted and knelt before me in mockery, yelling, "Hail! King of the Jews!"

And they hit me with their fists. They spit on me and grabbed the stick and beat me on the head with it. When they were finally tired of mocking me, they took off the robe and put my own clothes on me again.

Then they led me away to be crucified.

Mt. 27:11-31; Mk. 15:2-20; Lu. 23:1-25; Jo. 18:28-19:13, 15-16

PART VII

MY DEATH
AND
RESURRECTION

I

WAS

CRUCIFIED

APRIL 4, AD 30

The Crucifixion

So they took me and led me away, carrying the cross by myself. As we were on the way, we came across a man named Simon, who was from Cyrene, coming in from the country just then, and they forced him to follow me and carry my cross. (Simon is the father of Alexander and Rufus.)

Great crowds trailed along behind, including many grief-stricken women. But I turned and said to them, "Daughters of Jerusalem, don't weep for me, but weep for yourselves and for your children. For the days are coming when they will say, 'Fortunate indeed are the women who are childless, the wombs that have not borne a child and the breasts that have never nursed.' People will beg the mountains to fall on them and the hills to bury them. For if these things are done when the tree is green, what will happen when it is dry?"

Two others, both criminals, were led out to be executed with me. Finally, we came to a place called Golgotha (which in Hebrew means Skull Hill). There they crucified me.

9 AM

It was nine o'clock in the morning when the crucifixion took place.

The soldiers gave me wine drugged with myrrh, which is a bitter gall, but when I tasted it, I refused to drink it. Then they nailed me to the cross and crucified me. I said, "Father, forgive these people, because they don't know what they are doing."

12 Noon

And Pilate posted a signboard on the cross above my head, announcing the charge against me. It read: "This is Jesus of Nazareth, the King of the Jews." The place where I was crucified was near the city; and the sign was written in Hebrew, Latin, and Greek, so that many people could read it. Then the leading priests said to Pilate, "Change it from 'The King of the Jews' to 'He said, I am King of the Jews.'" Pilate replied, "What I have written, I have written. It stays exactly as it is." It was now about noon of the day of preparation for the Passover. And Pilate said to the people, "Here is your King!"

Both criminals were crucified there with me. I was on the center cross, and the two others on either side of mine. And the Scripture was fulfilled that said,

He was counted among those who were rebels.

Isa. 53:12

303

After the soldiers had nailed me to the cross, they gambled for my clothes. Throwing dice to decide who would get them, they divided my clothes among the four of them. They also took my robe, but it was seamless, woven in one piece from the top. So they said, "Let's not tear it but throw dice to see who gets it." This fulfilled the Scripture that says,

> They divided my clothes among themselves and threw
> dice for my robe.

Ps. 22:18

So that is what they did. Then they sat around and kept guard as I hung there.

The crowd watched, and the leaders laughed and scoffed. And the people passing by shouted abuse, shaking their heads in mockery. "Ha! Look at you now!" they yelled at me. "So! You can destroy the Temple and rebuild it in three days, can you? Well then, if you are the Son of God, save yourself and come down from the cross!"

The leading priests, teachers of religious law, and the other leaders also mocked me. "He saved others," they scoffed, "but he can't save himself! So he's the king of Israel, is he? Let this king of Israel, this Messiah, save himself if he is really God's Chosen One, the Messiah, and we will believe in him! He trusted God—let God show his approval by delivering him! For he said, 'I am the Son of God.' Let him come down from the cross, so that we can see it and believe him."

The soldiers mocked me, too, by offering me a drink of sour wine. They called out to me, "If you are the King of the Jews, save yourself!"

One of the criminals hanging beside me also shouted the same insults at me and ridiculed me. He scoffed, "So you're the Messiah, are you? Prove it by saving yourself—and us, too, while you're at it!"

But the other criminal protested, "Don't you fear God even when you are dying? We deserve to die for our evil deeds, but this man hasn't done anything wrong." Then he said, "Jesus, remember me when you come into your Kingdom." And I replied, "I assure you, today you will be with me in paradise."

Standing near the cross were my mother, and my mother's sister, Mary (the wife of Clopas), and Mary Magdalene. When I saw my mother standing there beside the disciple I loved, I said to her, "Woman, he is your son." And I said to this disciple, "She is your mother." And from then on this disciple took her into his home.

At noon, darkness fell across the whole land until three o'clock. The light from the sun was gone.

Then, at that time, about three o'clock, I called out with a loud voice, "Eloi, Eloi, lama sabachthani?" which means, "My God, my God, why have you forsaken me?" Some of the bystanders misunderstood and thought I was calling for the prophet Elijah.

I knew that everything was now finished, and to fulfill the Scriptures I said, "I am thirsty." A jar of sour wine was sitting there, so one of them ran and soaked a sponge in it, put it on a hyssop branch, and held it up to my lips so I could drink.

But the rest said, "Leave him alone. Let's see whether Elijah will come and take him down and save him."

When I had tasted it, I shouted out again, and said, "It is finished!" Then I bowed my head, uttered another loud cry, and shouted, "Father, I entrust my spirit into your hands!"

And with those words I breathed my last and gave up my spirit.

When the captain of the Roman soldiers, who was handling the executions, and who stood facing me, saw what had happened and how I died, he praised God and exclaimed, "Surely this man was innocent."

At that moment the curtain in the Temple was torn in two, from top to bottom. The earth shook, rocks split apart, and tombs opened. The bodies of many godly men and women who had died were raised from the dead after my resurrection. They left the cemetery, went into the holy city of Jerusalem, and appeared to many people.

The Roman officer and the other soldiers at the crucifixion were terrified by the earthquake and all that had happened. They said, "Truly this was the Son of God!"

And when the crowd that came to see the crucifixion saw all that had happened, they went home in deep sorrow, beating their breasts. But my friends, including the women who had followed me from Galilee, stood at a distance watching, including Mary Magdalene, Mary (mother of James the younger and of Joseph), Salome, and Zebedee's wife, the mother of James and John. They had been followers of mine and had cared for me while I was in Galilee. Then they and many other women had come with me to Jerusalem.

The Jewish leaders didn't want the victims hanging there the next day, which was the Sabbath (and a very special Sabbath at that because it was Passover), so they asked Pilate to hasten the deaths by ordering our legs be broken. Then our bodies could be taken down.

So the soldiers came and broke the legs of the two men crucified with me. But when they came to me, they saw that I was dead already, so they didn't break my legs. One of the soldiers, however, pierced my side with a spear, and blood and water flowed out.

These things happened in fulfillment of the Scriptures that say,

Not one of his bones will be broken,

Exodus 12:46; Num. 9:12; Ps. 34:20

and

They will look on him whom they pierced.

Zech. 12:10

Mt. 27:32-56; Mk. 15:21-41; Lu 23:26-49; Jo. 19:14, 17-34, 36-37

I
WAS
BURIED
BEFORE SUNSET
APRIL 4, AD 30

My Burial

This all happened on the day of preparation the day before the Sabbath.

Afterward, as evening approached, Joseph, a rich man from Arimathea in Judea, who was one of my followers, went to Pilate and asked for my body. A good and righteous man, he was an honored member of the Jewish high council, but had not agreed with the decision and actions of the other religious leaders.

He had been a secret disciple of mine (because he feared the Jewish leaders), and had been waiting for the Kingdom of God to come. He gathered his courage and went to Pilate to ask permission to take my body down.

Pilate couldn't believe that I was already dead, so he called for the Roman military officer in charge and asked him. The officer confirmed the fact, and Pilate issued an order to release my body to him, and told Joseph he could have it.

When Pilate gave him permission, Joseph took my body down from the cross and took it away. Nicodemus, the man who had come to me at night, also came, bringing about seventy-five pounds of embalming ointment made from myrrh and aloes. Joseph bought a long sheet of linen cloth. Together they wrapped my body in the long linen cloth with spices, as is the Jewish custom of burial. This was done late in the afternoon.

The place of crucifixion was near a garden, where there was a new tomb—Joseph's own tomb, which had been carved out of rock and had never been used before. And so, because it was the day of preparation before the Passover, and since the tomb was close at hand, they laid me there. Then Joseph rolled a great stone across the entrance as he left.

As my body was taken away, the women from Galilee followed and saw the tomb where they placed my body. Both Mary Magdalene and the other Mary, the mother of Joseph, were sitting nearby watching. Then they went home and prepared spices and ointments to embalm me. But by the time they were finished it was the Sabbath, so they rested all day as required by the law.

Mt. 27:57-61; Mk. 15:42-47, 16:1; Lu. 23:50-56; Jo. 19:38-42

APRIL 5, AD 30

My Tomb Was Sealed

April 5, AD 30

The next day—the first day of the Passover ceremonies—the leading priests and Pharisees went to see Pilate. They told him, "Sir, we remember what that deceiver once said while he was still alive: 'After three days I will be raised from the dead.' So we request that you seal the tomb until the third day. This will prevent his disciples from coming and stealing his body and then telling everyone he came back to life! If that happens, we'll be worse off than we were at first." Pilate replied, "Take guards and secure it the best you can." So they sealed the tomb and posted guards to protect it.

Mt. 27:62-66

SUNDAY

APRIL 7, AD 30

I
ROSE FROM
THE DEAD
ON
SUNDAY MORNING
APRIL 7, AD 30

My Tomb Was Empty

Sunday at daybreak, April 7, AD 30

Very early Sunday morning, there was a great earthquake, because an angel of the Lord came down from heaven to the tomb and rolled aside the stone and sat on it. His face shone like lightning, and his clothing was as white as snow. The guards shook when they saw him, and they fell into a dead faint.

While it was still dark, Mary Magdalene came to the tomb and found that the stone had been rolled away from the entrance. She ran and found Simon Peter and the other disciple, the one whom I loved. She said, "They have taken the Lord's body out of the tomb, and I don't know where they have put him!"

Peter and the other disciple ran to the tomb to see. The other disciple outran Peter and got there first. He stooped and looked in and saw the linen cloth lying there, but he didn't go in. Then Simon Peter arrived and went inside. He also noticed the linen wrappings lying there, while the cloth that had covered my head was folded up and lying to the side. Then the other disciple also went in, and he saw and believed—for until then they hadn't realized that the Scriptures said that he would rise from the dead. Then they went home.

Mary was standing outside the tomb crying, and as she wept, she stooped and looked in. She saw two white-robed angels sitting at the head and the foot of the place where my body had been lying. "Why are you crying?" the angels asked her.

"Because they have taken away my Lord," she replied, "and I don't know where they have put him."

She glanced over her shoulder and saw someone standing behind her. It was I, but she didn't recognize me. "Why are you crying?" I asked her. "Who are you looking for?"

She thought I was the gardener. "Sir," she said, "if you have taken him away, tell me where you have put him, and I will go and get him."

"Mary!" I said.

She turned toward me and exclaimed, "Teacher!"

"Don't cling to me," I said, "for I haven't yet ascended to the Father. But go find my brothers and tell them that I am ascending to my Father and your Father, my God and your God."

Mary Magdalene, the woman from whom I had cast out seven demons, was the first person who saw me when I rose from the dead.

Mary Magdalene found the disciples, who were grieving and weeping, and told them, "I have seen the Lord!" Then she gave them my message. But when she told them that I was alive and she had seen me, they didn't believe her.

Just at sunrise Joanna and Salome, Mary the mother of James, and the other Mary went out to the tomb, taking the burial spices they had purchased and prepared. On the way they were discussing who would roll the stone away from the entrance of the tomb. But when they arrived, they looked up and saw that the stone—a very large one—had already been rolled aside. So they went in, but they couldn't find my body. They were puzzled, trying to think what could have happened to it.

There on the right sat a young man clothed in a white robe. Suddenly, two men clothed in dazzling robes appeared to them. The women were terrified and bowed low before them, but the angel said, "Don't be afraid! I know you are looking for Jesus, who was crucified." Then the two men asked, "Why are you looking in a tomb for someone who is alive? He isn't here! He has risen from the dead just as he said!" The women were startled. But the angel said, "Do not be so surprised. Don't you remember what he told you back in Galilee, that the Son of Man must be betrayed into the hands of sinful men and be crucified, and that he would rise again on the third day?" Then the women remembered that I had said this.

"Come, see where his body was lying," he said. "And now, go quickly and tell his disciples, including Peter: Jesus has been raised from the dead. He is going ahead of you to Galilee. You will see him there, just as he told you before he died! Remember, I have told you."

The women fled from the tomb, and rushed to find the disciples to give them the angels' message. They ran quickly, trembling and bewildered, saying nothing to anyone because they were too frightened to talk.

And as they went, I met them. "Greetings!" I said. And they ran to me, held my feet, and worshiped me. Then I told them, "Don't be afraid! Go tell my brothers to leave for Galilee, and they will see me there." So they rushed back to tell my eleven disciples— and everyone else—what had happened. Filled with great joy, they reported all these instructions briefly to Peter and his companions. They told the apostles what had happened, but the story sounded like nonsense, so they didn't believe it. However, Peter ran to the tomb to look. Stooping, he peered in and saw the empty linen wrappings; then he went home again, wondering what had happened.

As the women were on their way into the city, some of the men who had been guarding the tomb went to the leading priests and told them what had happened. A meeting of all the religious leaders was called, and they decided to bribe the soldiers. They told the soldiers, "You must say, 'Jesus' disciples came during the night while we were sleeping, and they stole his body.' If the governor hears about it, we'll stand up for you and everything will be all right." So the guards accepted the bribe and said what they were told to say. Their story spread widely among the Jews, and they still tell it today.

Mt. 28:1-15; Mk. 16:2-8b, 9-11; Lu. 24:1-12; Jo. 20:1-18

Several People Saw Me

Sunday afternoon-evening

Afterward, that same day, I appeared to two of my followers who were walking from Jerusalem into the country, to the village of Emmaus, seven miles out of Jerusalem.

As they walked along they were talking about everything that had happened. Suddenly, I myself came along and joined them and began walking beside them. But they didn't know who I was, because God kept them from recognizing me.

"You seem to be in a deep discussion about something," I said. "What are you so concerned about?"

They stopped short, sadness written across their faces. Then one of them, Cleopas, replied, "You must be the only person in Jerusalem who hasn't heard about all the things that have happened there the last few days."

"What things?" I asked.

"The things that happened to Jesus, the man from Nazareth," they said. "He was a prophet who did wonderful miracles. He was a mighty teacher, highly regarded by both God and all the people. But our leading priests and other religious leaders arrested him and handed him over to be condemned to death, and they crucified him. We had thought he was the Messiah who had come to rescue Israel. That all happened three days ago.

"Then some women from our group of his followers were at his tomb early this morning, and they came back with an amazing report. They said his body was missing, and they had seen angels who told them Jesus is alive! Some of our men ran out to see, and sure enough, Jesus' body was gone, just as the women had said."

Then I said to them, "You are such foolish people! You find it so hard to believe all that the prophets wrote in the Scriptures. Wasn't it clearly predicted by the prophets that the Messiah would have to suffer all these things before entering his time of glory?" Then I quoted passages from the writings of Moses and all the prophets, explaining what all the Scriptures said about me.

By this time we were nearing Emmaus and the end of their journey. I would have gone on, but they begged me to stay the night with them, since it was getting late. So I went home with them.

As we sat down to eat, I took a small loaf of bread, asked God's blessing on it, broke it, then gave it to them. Suddenly, their eyes were opened, and they recognized me. And at that moment I disappeared!

They said to each other, "Didn't our hearts feel strangely warm as he talked with us on the road and explained the Scriptures to us?"

And within the hour they were on their way back to Jerusalem, where the eleven disciples and my followers gathered.

That evening, on the first day of the week, the disciples were meeting behind locked doors because they were afraid of the Jewish leaders. When the two arrived, they were greeted with the report, "The Lord has really risen! He appeared to Peter!"

Then the two from Emmaus told their story of how I had appeared to them as they were walking along the road and how they had recognized me as I was breaking the bread, but no one believed them. And just as they were telling about it, I myself was suddenly standing there among them!

I rebuked them for their unbelief—their stubborn refusal to believe those who had seen me after I had risen. But the whole group was terribly frightened, thinking they were seeing a ghost! "Peace be with you." I said.

"Why are you frightened?" I asked. "Why do you doubt who I am? Look at my hands. Look at my feet. You can see that it is really I. Touch me and make sure that I am not a ghost, because ghosts don't have bodies, as you see that I do!" As I spoke, I held out my hands for them to see, and I showed them my feet and side. I spoke to them again and said, "Peace be with you. As the Father has sent me, so I send you." Then I breathed on them and said to them, "Receive the Holy Spirit. If you forgive anyone's sins, they are forgiven. If you refuse to forgive them, they are unforgiven."

Still they stood there doubting, filled with joy and wonder! Then I asked them, "Do you have anything here to eat?" They gave me a piece of broiled fish, and I ate it as they watched.

One of the disciples, Thomas (nicknamed the Twin), was not with the others when I came. They told him, "We have seen the Lord!" But he replied, "I will not believe it unless I see the nail wounds in his hands, put my fingers into them, and place my hand into the wound in his side."

Then the eleven disciples left for Galilee, going to the mountain where I had told them to go.

Mt. 28:16; Mk. 16:12-13, 14b; Lu. 24:13-43; Jo. 20:19-25

PART VIII

MY
LAST DAYS
ON EARTH

I
MET MY DISCIPLES
IN GALILEE
MONDAY
APRIL 15, AD 30

Thomas No Longer Doubted

Monday, April 15, AD 30   Galilee

Eight days later the disciples were together again, and this time Thomas was with them. The doors were locked; but suddenly, as before, I was standing among them. I said, "Peace be with you." When they saw me, they worshiped me—but some still doubted.

Then I said to Thomas, "Put your finger here and see my hands. Put your hand into the wound in my side. Don't be faithless any longer. Believe!"

"My Lord and my God!" Thomas exclaimed. Then I told him, "You believe because you have seen me. Blessed are those who haven't seen me and believe anyway."

Mt. 28:17; Jo. 20:26-29

I Again Appeared to My Disciples

April-May, AD 30   The Sea of Galilee

Later I appeared again to the disciples beside the Sea of Galilee. This is how it happened. Several of the disciples were there—Simon Peter, Thomas (nicknamed the Twin), Nathanael from Cana in Galilee, the sons of Zebedee, and two other disciples.

Simon Peter said, "I'm going fishing."

"We'll come, too," they all said. So they went out in the boat, but they caught nothing all night.

At dawn the disciples saw me standing on the beach, but they couldn't see who I was. I called out, "Friends, have you caught any fish?"

"No," they replied.

Then I said, "Throw out your net on the right-hand side of the boat, and you'll get plenty of fish!" So they did, and they couldn't draw in the net because there were so many fish in it.

Then the disciple whom I loved said to Peter, "It is the Lord!"

When Simon Peter heard that it was I, the Lord, he put on his tunic (for he had stripped for work), jumped into the water, and swam ashore. The others stayed with the boat and pulled the loaded net to the shore, for they were only out about three hundred feet. When they got there, they saw that a charcoal fire was burning and fish were frying over it, and there was bread.

"Bring some of the fish you've just caught," I said. So Simon Peter went aboard and dragged the net to the shore. There were 153 large fish, and yet the net hadn't torn.

"Now come and have some breakfast!" I said. And no one dared ask me if I really was the Lord because they were sure of it. Then I served them the bread and the fish.

This was the third time I had appeared to my disciples since I had been raised from the dead.

Jo. 21:1-14

I Asked Peter if He Really Loved Me

After breakfast I came and said to Simon Peter, "Simon son of John, do you love me more than these?"

"Yes, Lord," Peter replied, "you know I love you."

"Then feed my lambs," I told him. I repeated the question: "Simon son of John, do you love me?"

"Yes, Lord," Peter said, "you know I love you."

"Then take care of my sheep," I said.

Once more I asked him, "Simon son of John, do you love me?"

Peter was grieved that I asked the question a third time. He said, "Lord, you know everything. You know I love you."

I said, "Then feed my sheep.

"The truth is, when you were young, you were able to do as you liked and go wherever you wanted to. But when you are old, you will stretch out your hands, and others will direct you and take you where you don't want to go." I said this to let him know what kind of death he would die to glorify God. Then I told him, "Follow me."

Peter turned around and saw the disciple I loved following us—the one who had leaned over to me during supper and asked, "Lord, who among us will betray you?" Peter asked me, "What about him. Lord?" I replied, "If I want him to remain alive until I return, what is that to you? You follow me." So the rumor spread among the community of believers that that disciple wouldn't die. But that isn't what I said at all. I only said, "If I want him to remain alive until I return, what is that to you?"

Jo. 21:15-23

I
COMMISSIONED
MY
DISCIPLES

I Commissioned My Disciples to Spread the Good News Concerning Me

Still later I appeared to the eleven disciples as they were eating together. And then I said to them, "Go into all the world and preach the Good News to everyone, everywhere. Anyone who believes and is baptized will be saved. But anyone who refuses to believe will be condemned. These signs will accompany those who believe: They will cast out demons in my name, and they will speak new languages. They will be able to handle snakes with safety, and if they drink anything poisonous, it won't hurt them. They will be able to place their hands on the sick and heal them."

Then I told my disciples, "I have been given complete authority in heaven and on earth. Therefore, go and make disciples of all nations, baptizing them in the name of the Father and the Son and the Holy Spirit. Teach these new disciples to obey all the commands I have given you. And be sure of this: I am with you always, even to the end of the age."

Then I said, "When I was with you before, I told you that everything written about me by Moses and the prophets and in the Psalms must all come true." Then I opened their minds to understand these many Scriptures. And I said, "Yes, it was written long ago that the Messiah must suffer and die and rise again from the dead on the third day.

"With my authority, take this message of repentance to all the nations, beginning in Jerusalem: 'There is forgiveness of sins for all who turn to me.'"

(Later, I myself sent the disciples out from east to west with the sacred and unfailing message of salvation that gives eternal life. They went everywhere and preached, and I worked with them, confirming what they said by many miraculous signs.)

"You are witnesses of all these things. And now I will send the Holy Spirit, just as my Father promised. But stay in the city until the Holy Spirit comes and fills you with power from heaven."

Mt. 28:18-20; Mk. 16:8c, 14a, 15-18, 20; Lu. 24:44-49

I
ASCENDED
TO MY
FATHER
MAY 14, AD 30

I Ascended

May 14, AD 30   Bethany

Then I led them to Bethany, and lifting my hands to heaven, I blessed them.

While I was blessing them, I left them and was taken up to heaven and sat down in the place of honor at God's right hand.

The disciples worshiped me and then they returned to Jerusalem filled with great joy. And they spent time in the Temple praising God.

Mk. 16:19; Lu. 24:50-53

THERE
WERE WITNESSES
TO ALL THESE
THINGS

Luke's Witness

Most honorable Theophilus, many people have written accounts of the events that have taken place among us. They used as their source material the reports circulating among us from the early disciples and other eye witnesses of what God has done in fulfillment of his promises. Having carefully investigated all of these accounts from the beginning, I have decided to write a careful summary for you to reassure you of the truth of all you were taught.

Luke 1:1-4

Luke

John's Witness

We have all benefited from the rich blessings he brought to us—one gracious blessing after another. For the law was given through Moses; God's unfailing love and faithfulness came through Jesus Christ. No one has ever seen God. But his only Son, who is himself God, is near to the Father's heart; he has told us about him.

John 1:16-18

John

This report is from an eyewitness giving an accurate account; it is presented so that you also can believe.

John 19:35

John

We disciples saw him do many other miraculous signs besides the ones recorded in this book. But these are written so that you might believe that Jesus is the Messiah, the Son of God, and that by believing in him you will have life. Amen.

John 20:30-31

John

This is that disciple who saw these events, and recorded them here. And we all know that this account of these things is accurate. And I suppose that if all the other things Jesus did were written down, the whole world could not contain the books.

John 21:24-25

John

End Notes

Page

45 *Mark states that Jesus, himself, saw the dove, while Matthew and Luke are not specific.

71 *Peter and Andrew are mentioned earlier (John 1:35-51). Andrew was a follower of John the Baptist when Jesus met the brothers for the first time. Jesus now called them to be his disciples (see page 50).

79 *Matthew is also called Levi (Luke 5:27, 29).

91 *Bartholomew is believed to be Nathanael's surname.
     **Thaddaeus is also called Judas (Luke 6:16).

98 *Or: "for God will treat you as you treat others"; Greek reads "for with the judgement you judge, you will be judged."

99 *Or: "is fully trained."

107 *Some manuscripts do not include "and sisters."

112 *Or: "things new and old."

113 *Or: "mystery."
     **Or: "For whoever has, to him shall be given, and he shall have abundance; but whoever does not have, even what he has shall be taken away from him."

114: *Or: "the man who hears the Word and understands it."

117 *The Gerasenes are also called Gadarenes (Matthew 8:28).

139 *Or: "let the children eat first."

140 *Dalmanutha is also called Magadan (Matthew 15:37).

143 *Or: "shelters." The Greek reads "tabernacles."

160 *Or: "if you abide in my Word."

161 *Or: "he must work the works of Him who sent me."

164 *Or: "the Festival of Dedication."

177 *Or: "deeply moved in spirit."

183 *Or: "Levite."

190 *Or: "the sons of light."

202 *Or: "These things the nations of the world eagerly seek."

Scripture Reference Guide

MATTHEW	MARK	LUKE	JOHN
	1:1		
			1:1-5, 10-14
		1:5-25	
1:18b-25		1:26-38	
		1:39-56	
		1:57-80	1:6-9
1:18a, 2:1a		**2:1-21**	
		2:22-38	
2:1b-12		**2:39**	
2:13-23		2:40	
		2:41-52	
1:1-17			
		3:23b-38	
3:1-12	1:2-8	3:1-18	
3:13-17	**1:9-11**	**3:21-22,4:1a**	
4:1-11	1:12-13	4:1b-13	
			1:15, 19-34
			1:35-51
		3:23a	**2:1-12**
			2:13-25
			3:1-21
			3:22-36
		3:19-20	
4:12	1:14a		4:1-42
4:13-17	**1:14b-15**	**4:14a,31a**	**4:43-45**
			4:46-54
		4:14b-30	

345

Page

346

MATTHEW	MARK	LUKE	JOHN
4:18-22	**1:16-20**		
4:23-25			
	1:21-28	**4:31b-37**	
8:14-17	1:29-39	4:38-44	
9:35-38			
		5:1-11	
8:2-4	**1:40-45**	**5:12-16**	
9:1-8	2:1-12	5:17-26	
9:9-13	**2:13-17**	**5:27-32**	
9:14-17	2:18-22	5:33-39	
			5:1-47
12:1-15	2:23-3:6	6:1-11	
10:1b-4	**3:13-19**	**6:12-16**	
12:16-21	3:7-12	6:17-19	
5:1-12		**6:20-26**	
5:13-6:4		6:27-36	
6:5-24			
6:25-7:6		6:37-42	
7:7-29		**6:43-49**	
8:1,5-13		7:1-10	
		7:11-17	
11:2-19		7:18-35	
		7:36-50	
		8:1-3	
12:22-37	**3:20-30**	**11:14-15, 17-23, 33-36**	
		11:37-54	
12:38-46	**3:31-32a, 4:21-25**	**8:16-19, 11:16, 24-32**	
12:47-50	3:32b-35	8:20-21	
13:24-52	**4:10a, 26-34**		
13:1-23	4:1-9,10b-20	8:4-15	
8:18, 23-27	**4:35-41**	**8:22-25**	
8:28-34	5:1-20	8:26-39	
9:18-26	**5:21-43**	**8:40-56**	
9:27-34			
10:1a, 5-11:1	**6:6b-13**	**9:1-6**	
14:1-13a	**6:14-29**	**9:7-9**	
14:13b-23	6:30-46	9:10-17	6:1-17a

347

MATTHEW	MARK	LUKE	JOHN
14:24-39	**6:47-56**		**6:17b-21**
			6:22-7:1
15:1-20	**7:1-23**		
15:21-28	7:24-30		
	7:31-37		
15:29-37	8:1-10		
16:1-12	**8:11-21**		
	8:22-26		
16:13-28	**8:27-9:1**	**9:18-27**	
17:1-13	9:2-13	9:28-36	
17:14-21	**9:14-29**	**9:37-43a**	
17:22-35	9:30-32	9:43b-45	
18:1-35	**9:33-50**	**9:46-50**	
	10:1a		7:2-10
		10:38-42	
			7:11-36
			7:37-53
			8:1-11
			8:12-59
			9:1-41
			10:1-21
			10:22-42
		11:1-13	
			11:1-54
13:53b-58	**6:1-6a**		
11:20-30		10:1-24	
		10:25-37	
		14:1-6	
		14:7-16:17,19-17:10	
8:19-22		9:51-62	
		17:11-19	
		17:20-37	
		18:1-14	
13:53a, 19:1-12	10:1b-12	16:18	
19:13-15	**10:13-16**	**18:15-17**	
19:16-26	10:17-27	18:18-27	
19:27-20:16	**10:28-31**	**18:28-30**	

Page

MATTHEW	MARK	LUKE	JOHN
		12:1-13:9	
		13:10-21	
20:17-19, 23:37-39	**10:32-34**	**13:22-35, 18:31-34**	
20:20-28	10:35-45		
20:29b-30		**18:35-43**	
	10:46a	19:1-10	
20:29a, 31-34	**10:46b-52**		
		19:11-28	
26:6-13	**14:3-9**		**11:55-12:11**
21:1-11	11:1-11	19:29-44	12:12-19
21:19-19a	**11:12-14**		
21:12-17	11:15-19	19:45-48	
21:19b-22	**11:20-26**		
21:23-22:14	11:27-12:12	20:1-19	
22:15-22	**12:13-17**	**20:20-26**	
22:23-33	12:18-27	20:27-40	
22:34-46	**12:28-37**	**20:41-44**	
	12:38-40	20:45-47	
	12:41-44	**21:1-4**	
23:1-36			
			12:20-50
24:1-51	13:1-37	21:5-38	
25:1-46			
26:1-5,14-16	14:1-2,10-11	22:1-6	
26:17-20	**14:12-17**	**22:7-18**	**13:1-2**
			13:3-20
26:21-29	**14:18-25**	**22:19-30**	**13:21-38**
			14:1-31
			15:1-16:33
			17:1-28
26:30-35	**14:26-31**	**22:31-39**	
26:36-46	14:32-42	22:40-46	18:1
26:47-56	**14:43-52**	**22:47-53**	**18:2-11**
26:57-68	14:53-65	22:54-55,63-65	18:12-16,18-24

PAGE

MATTHEW	MARK	LUKE	JOHN
26:69-75	**14:66-72**	**22:56-62**	**18:17,25-27**
27:1-2	15:1	22:66-71	
27:3-10			
27:11-31	15:2-20	23:1-25	18:28-19:13,15-16
27:32-56	**15:21-41**	**23:26-49**	**19:14, 17-34, 36-37**
27:57-61	15:42-47, 16:1	23:50-56	19:38-42
27:62-66			
28:1-15	16:2-8b, 9-11	24:1-12	20:1-18
28:16	**16:112-13,14b**	**24:13-43**	**20:19-25**
28:17			**20:26-29**
			21:1-14
			21:15-23
	16:8c, 14a		
28:18-20	15-18,20	24:44-49	
	16:19	**24:50-53**	
		1:1-4	
			1:16-18,19:35,
			20:30-31, 21:24-25

Revolutionary Bible Study

"One of the most important books I will ever write."

The letters in your New Testament are arranged in a chaotic order. That happened in about 200 A.D. Some 1800 years later, the letters are still in chaos.

Until Revolutionary Bible Study, no one attempted to show us what happened in Century One in the order in which the events happened.

Revolutionary Bible Study tells you those events...30–70 A.D., year by year. For the first time, you will know the year and the context of the New Testament—that is, all the important events.

Unleashing the Word of God

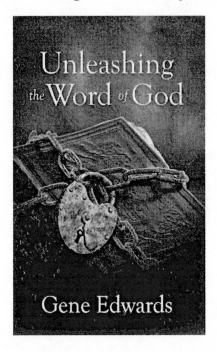

DVD Included

The DVD will shock you. It will prove without question why we cannot possibly understand the New Testament until we rearrange the epistles into their proper order. We presently work our way through the letters in a jumbled maze when we could read it on a straight super highway. You and I have never, do not, and cannot understand the New Testament. Think that statement is impossible? Wait until you see the DVD. We have not grasped the New Testament in its great panoramic scene because of the bizarre way the epistles are arranged.

Read *Unleashing the Work of God* and *Revolutionary Bible Study*. You will unleash the Scripture, and it will be a revolution. The chart you see in the DVD will show the sheer impossibility of having a clear sight of the Scripture the way it is presently arranged.

SeedSowers

Christian Books Publishing House
PO Box 3317 ● 4003 N. Liberty St.
Jacksonville, FL 32206
SeedSowers.com

1-800- ACT BOOK
1-800-228-2665

NEW

	Author
I, Jeanne Guyon	*James*
The Jeanne Guyon Nobody Knows	*Edwards*
Here's How to Win Souls	*Edwards*

SPIRITUAL CLASSICS

Experiencing the Depths of Jesus Christ	*Guyon*
Practicing His Presence	*Lawrence/Laubach*
Spiritual Guide	*Molinos*
The Seeking Heart	*Fenelon*
Intimacy with Christ	*Guyon*
Song of Songs	*Guyon*
Final Steps in Christian Maturity	*Guyon*
Spiritual Torrents	*Guyon*
Union with God	*Guyon*

THREE CLASSICS BY ONE AUTHOR

A Tale of Three Kings	*Edwards*
The Divine Romance	*Edwards*
Prisoner in the Third Cell	*Edwards*

INTRODUCTION TO THE DEEPER CHRISTIAN LIFE

Living by the Highest Life	*Edwards*
Secret to the Christian Life	*Edwards*
Inward Journey	*Edwards*

THE CHRONICLES OF HEAVEN

The Beginning	*Edwards*
The Escape	*Edwards*
The Birth	*Edwards*
The Triumph	*Edwards*
The Return	*Edwards*

THE FIRST-CENTURY DIARIES

The Silas Diary	*Edwards*
The Titus Diary	*Edwards*
The Timothy Diary	*Edwards*
The Priscilla Diary	*Edwards*
The Gaius Diary	*Edwards*

DEVOTIONAL

100 Days in the Secret Place	*Edwards*
Living Close to God (When You're Not Good at It)	*Edwards*

COMFORT AND HEALING

Healing for Christians Who Have Been Crucified by Christians	*Edwards*
Letters to a Devastated Christian	*Edwards*
Dear Lillian	*Edwards*
Suffering	*Pradhan*

BOOKS ON CHURCH LIFE

Climb the Highest Mountain	*Edwards*
How to Meet in Homes	*Edwards*
The Organic Church vs the "New Testament Church"	*Edwards*
The Christian Woman Set Free	*Edwards*

OLD TESTAMENT

Guyon's Commentaries	*Guyon*

Genesis ● Exodus ● Leviticus-Numbers-Deuteronomy ● Judges ● Jeremiah

NEW TESTAMENT

Story of My Life, as Told by Jesus Christ	*The Gospels*
Your Lord Is a Blue Collar Worker	*Edwards*
The Day I Was Crucified	*Edwards*
Revolution, The Story of the Early Church	*Edwards*
Revolutionary Bible Study	*Edwards*
Unleashing the Word of God	*Edwards*
Acts in First Person	*The Book of Acts*

CHURCH HISTORY

Torch of the Testimony	*Kennedy*
Going to Church in the First Century	*Banks*
Passing of the Torch	*Chen*
When the Church Was Led Only by Laymen	*Edwards*
When the Church Was Young	*Loosley*

BIOGRAPHIES

I, Jeanne Guyon	*James*
Prem Pradhan, Apostle to Nepal	*Pradhan*
The Jeanne Guyon Nobody Knows	*Edwards*

EVANGELISM

Here's How to Win Souls	*Edwards*

RADICAL LITERATURE

How Paul Trained Men	*Edwards*
Are We Really Being Biblical?	*Edwards*
God Is Looking for a Man for the 21st Century	*Edwards*
Americanization of Christianity	*Edwards*
Concerning Our Missions	*Nee*

CPSIA information can be obtained
at www.ICGtesting.com
Printed in the USA
FSOW02n1426290317
32452FS